TOURIST ATLAS OF BEIJING

DADI CORPORATION OF THE INSTITUTE OF GEOGRAPHY,
CHINESE ACADEMY OF SCIENCES

BEIJING　　　　TOURISM　　　　ADMINISTRATION

SCIENCE PRESS, BEIJING, CHINA

1990

First published 1990
ISBN 7−03−002058−8 / G · 155 (外)

To offer All-round Service to Tourists

——Congratulations on the Publication of the *Tourist Atlas of Beijing*

On the occasion of the publication of the *Tourist Atlas of Beijing*, I wish to extend my thanks to all the researchers of the Institute of Geography of the Chinese Academy of Sciences for the good service they have rendered to the development of tourism by making use of their expertise.

Beijing, the capital of China, is a city of a long history. As the ancient capital of five dynasties — the Liao, Jin, Yuan, Ming and Qing — it boasts numerous historical relics and beautiful scenery, which offer great attraction to tourists the world over. After ten years of development of tourism, Beijing now claims to be basically complete with various kinds of tourist installations and services. All this no doubt constitutes its advantage as a tourist city. However, this alone will not suffice, for there is a need yet to be met — to provide tourists with consulting services — and the publication of the atlas represents a step forward in this direction. Now that an atlas is available, friends abroad can get the necessary advice and guidance when making tour plans for Beijing, choosing touring routes and deciding places for a visit; in short, they can expect convenient consulting service whether they visit Beijing for sightseeing, for business talks or on other professional tours.

I sincerely hope that the atlas will help friends from abroad deepen their knowledge of Beijing and perpetuate their happy memory of the city.

Bo Xicheng
Director of Tourism Administration of Beijing

Foreword

Beijing, famous for its long history and culture, is the capital of China, one of the tourist centers of the country and a well-known tourist city of the world. It is held in respect by all the nationalities in China, and is attracting more and more tourists from different parts of the world. With the development of tourism in Beijing, there is an ever great need to know its history and culture, environment, scenic spots and tourist services and installations. It is for the purpose of meeting this need that this atlas —*Tourist Atlas of Beijing* — is compiled.

This atlas features mainly tourist maps. However, to provide a complete picture of Beijing as a tourist city for ready reference by tourists, it also includes photographs, tables, picture captions and an index of place names. In designing and compiling the atlas, efforts have been made to achieve an integration of knowledge, artistry and practicality, and to embody the following features:

1. For each scenic spot, the most suitable form of picture is supplied, which can best reflect its relationship with the natural environment and give a strong sense of truthfulness. The picture may be a bird's-eye view, an aerial photograph, a sketch, a plan, or whatever, as called for by the characteristics of the natural and human landscape of the spot. For instance, aerial photographs are chosen for Tian'anmen Square and the Imperial Palace Museum, because aerial photographs give the fullest possible reflection of the grandeur of the square and symmetrical structure of the ancient palace; oblique perspective coloured maps are chosen for the two scenic spots — Fragrant Hills and the Ming Tombs — because these maps are able to show their different locations and produce better three-dimensional effects.

2. A caption is prepared for each scenic spot, explaining in simple terms its history, formation and features for the purpose of widening the tourists' scope of knowledge and enhancing their interest.

3. Coloured pictures, including many aerial photographs, are supplied for the scenic spots with a view of giving tourists a clear depiction and an overall picture of the places of interest they are to visit.

It is hoped that the atlas, with its rich collection of pictures and ingeniously written captions, will serve as a useful guide to tourists, helping them enjoy the beauty of nature and historical relics, and at the same time acquire knowledge of natural and human geography on their happy and relaxed tours.

The compilers wish to acknowledge their debt to the Geological Remote Sensing Center of the Chnese Academy of Sciences for the use of its aerial photographs, China Map Press for the use of its maps, and other departments for their publications which are either quoted from or referred to in the preparation of the atlas. Thanks are also extended to Zhang Chengxuan, Cai Zhengyi, Xu Jingfang, Gu Xuezai, Sun Zhongming, Cao Likun, Zheng Ping, Zhang Li and Qiu Fuke for their warm-hearted support and service.

Qian Jinkai

LEGEND

	Street; Residential Quarter		○	Tourist Service
⊙	Municipal Government		◑	Guesthouse; Hotel
◎	District Government		♀	Restaurant
○	Subdistrict Office		▮	Theatre
	District Border		▦	Cinema
	Railway		◐	Library; Museum; Former Residence
	Highway		♯	Cultural and Historic Site
	Airline		🏯 🏯	Temple
	River; Perennial River		⛩ ▮	Tower; Pavilion
	Seasonal River		▭	Gymnasium
	Lake		⊕	Hospital
	The Grand Canal		◉	Bank
	Reservoir		• •	Company; Shop
	The Great Wall		卍	Post Office
▲ 8848	Mountain Peak and Elevation		✿	Factory
	Famous Architecture		♈	Railway Booking Office
★	Government Office		✈	CAAC Booking Office
◎	Scientific Research Institution		🚌	The Centre Station of Long-distance Bus
⊛	University and College		🚕	TAXI Station
•	News and Press			Motor Line

A Guide to the Tourist Landscapes of Beijing

The Tourist Service Facilities of Beijing

The Maps of 24 Scenic Spots in Beijing

NTS

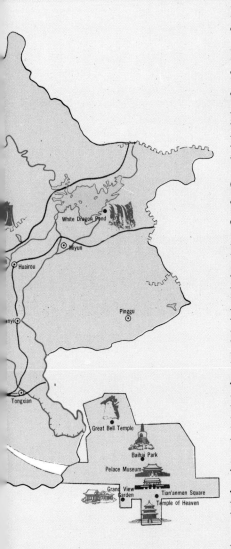

SCENIC SPOTS IN BEIJING
AND ITS ADJACENT AREAS

Eight Outer Temples at Summer Mountain Resort

Potala Temple
Temple of Special Image of Buddha
The Temple of Universal Tranquility
Temple of Universal Blessing
Temple of Universal Happiness and Longevity
The Temple of Simeru Happiness and Longevity
Mahayana Hall
Temple of Tranquilize Remote
Club Hill
Eight Outer Temples The Temple of Universal Happiness
Temple of Universal Humanity

Chengde

Snow Accumulated on Nanshan Mountain

Summer Mountain Resort

Main Palace

The First Pass of the World

Shanhaiguan Pass

Nanyuan

Shanhaiguan Railway Station

Temple of Maiden Meng Jian

The Great Wall

0   13

2116m
Mountain
Reserve   81

Tomb of Shou Prince

Yingshouyingzi

26

Dushan Mt. 1846m

Qinglong

Laolongtou
(Old Dragon's Head)

Xinglong

Yanfei Mountain
1142m

Wall at
...guan

The   Great   Wall

Eastern Qing
...nasty Mausoleum

12   13   23   11

Zhunhua

LURUI MT.

Qingdongling
Eastern Tomb   Xiaoling
Tomb   Xiaodong
Tomb

Dingling
Tomb   Yuling
Tomb   Juoling
Tomb

9   13

28

...on Reservoir

33   Yutian

32   Fengrun

45

Qianxi

Qian'an

The   Great   Wall

Laocen Hill
1424m
Laocen Natural
Landscapes
Beiniu Peak

Mount Nanshan
923m

Yansai Lake

Xuanyang Cave

17   Shanhai Pass

20   Qinhuangdao

71

Lulong

Funing

12   11

13   4

11

Guye

Luanxian

34

Jieshi Mountain

Changli

26

8   Beidaihe River

Guayue Peak

Temple of
Supremacy

Zigai Peak

Shaolin Temple

...an Peak

...e of
Results

To Jixian County

Lianhua Ridge

23

27

Tangshan

Fengnan

48

33

Changli Golden Seaside

Qinhuangdao
Railway Station

Seamen's Club
Gangkou Club

Gangchi

Hedong Club

He Bei
Haibin Road
Wenhua Road

Cultural
Palace

45

Ninghe

Tanghai

Lianpengshan Park

Temple of
Avalokilesvara

...cheng

Hangu

Chaobai   River

Douhe   R.

Beidaihe Seaside Recuperating Area

Seaside Resort

Tiger
Stone

Liuzhuang

Chitu
Mountain

Yingjiao
Rock
(Geiziwo)

Dagang

Tanggu

Bohai   Bay

Jinshanzui

Lama
Road

Tianjin Railway Station

Department Store

Quonye Market

Laoxikai Church   Friendship Guesthouse

Tianjin Hotel

Jiefang
Road

Bohai   Sea

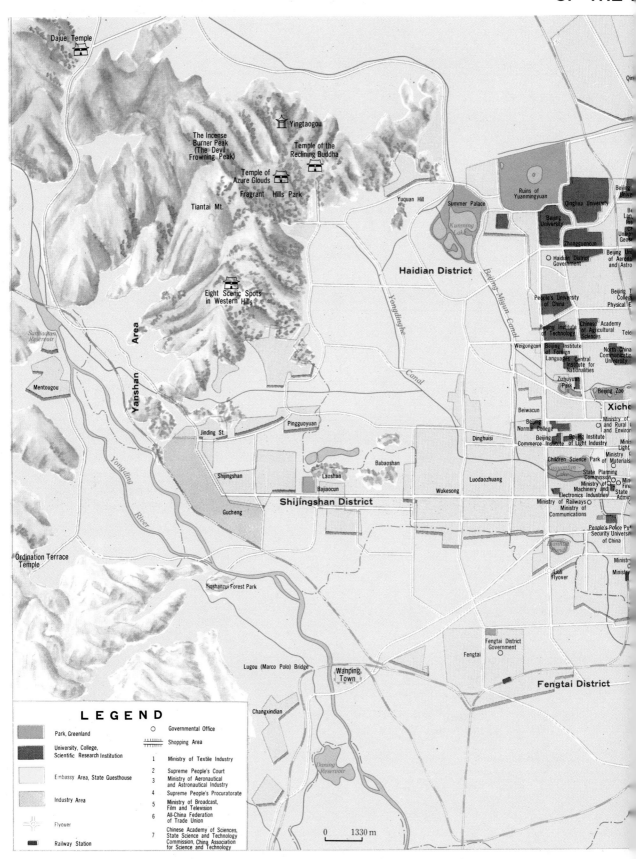

Dajue Temple

Yingtaogou

The Incense
Burner Peak
(The Devil
Frowning Peak)

Temple of the
Reclining Buddha

Temple of
Azure Clouds

Fragrant Hills Park

Tiantai Mt.

Yuquan Hill

Summer Palace

Kunming Lake

Ruins of
Yuanmingyuan

Qinghua University

Beijing
University

Beijing University

Zhongguancun

Haidian District
Government

Beijing Un
of Aerona
and Astro

Haidian District

Eight Scenic Spots
in Western Hills

People's University
of China

Beijing
Lan
In
Un
Geos

Beijing T
Colleg
Physical E

Yanshan

Area

Sanjiaqian
Reservoir

Beijing Institute
of Technology

Chinese Academy
of Agricultural
Sciences

Tele

Beijing-Miyun Canal

Yongdinghe

Canal

Mentougou

Beijing Institute
of Foreign
Languages
Institute for
Nationalities

North China
Communicatio
University

Weigongcun

Zizhuyuan
Park

Beijing Zoo

Beiwacun

Xiche

Jinding St.

Pingguoyuan

Beijing
Normal College

Beijing Institute
Commerce Institute of Light Industry

Ministry of
and Rural D
and Environ

Dinghuisi

Ministry
Light

Shijingshan

Laoshan

Babaoshan

Children Science Park of Materials

Ministry
Fine

Bajiaocun

Luodaozhuang

Wukesong

Yinanmian
Lake

State Planning
Commission

Ministry and In
Machinery and In
Electronics Industries

Min

State
Admin

Shijingshan District

Gucheng

Ministry of Railways
Ministry of
Communications

People's Police Pu
Security Universi
of China

Ministr
C

Ministr

Luli
Flyover

Kunming
Pond

Ordination Terrace
Temple

Yingshanzui Forest Park

Yongding

River

Lugou (Marco Polo) Bridge

Wanping
Town

Fengtai

Fengtai District
Government

Fengtai District

Changxindian

Daning
Reservoir

LEGEND

	Park, Greenland	○	Governmental Office
	University, College, Scientific Research Institution	⊥⊥⊥⊥	Shopping Area
	Embassy Area, State Guesthouse	1	Ministry of Textile Industry
	Industry Area	2	Supreme People's Court
		3	Ministry of Aeronautical and Astronautical Industry
	Flyover	4	Supreme People's Procuratorate
	Railway Station	5	Ministry of Broadcast, Film and Television
		6	All-China Federation of Trade Union
		7	Chinese Academy of Sciences, State Science and Technology Commission, China Association for Science and Technology

0   1330 m

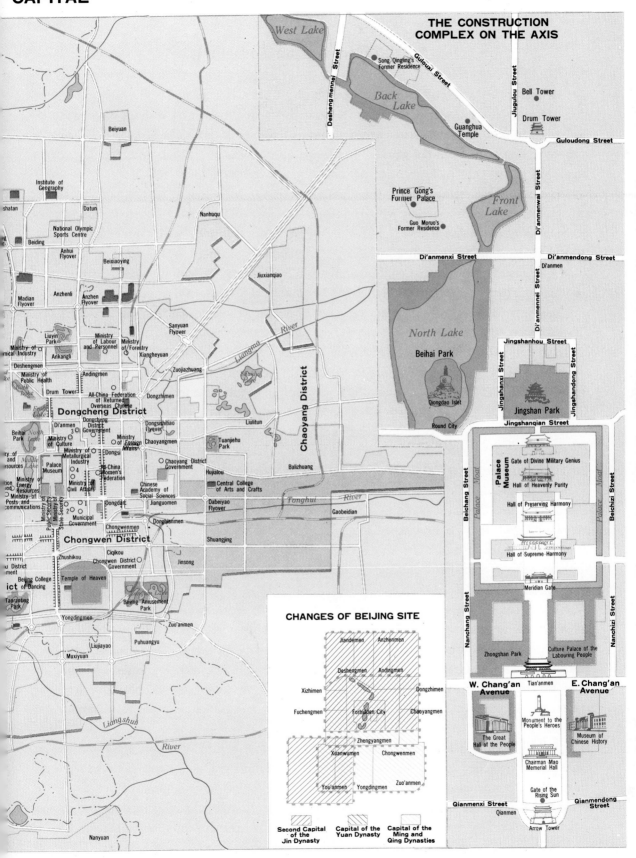

THE CONSTRUCTION
COMPLEX ON THE AXIS

CHANGES OF BEIJING SITE

Second Capital of the Jin Dynasty

Capital of the Yuan Dynasty

Capital of the Ming and Qing Dynasties

A Brief Introduction To Beijing

Beijing is the capital of the People's Republic of China. It is located at the northern rim of the extensive North China Plain, with the vast Bohai Sea in its east and the uninterrupted Taihang and Yanshan Mountains in its northwest, adjoining the Inner Mongolia Plateau. It was said "Best location in the world". The city is divided into 19 districts and counties, covers an area of 16,800 km^2 and comprises a population of over 10 millions.

Located on the warm-temperate, semihumid monsoon zone, Beijing is dominated by a typical continental monsoon climate with distinct seasons and comfortable weather. The annual average temperature in this area is 11.5℃. The coldest month is January with average temperature of −4.6℃ and the warmest is July, 25.8℃. The annual precipitation is 644.2 mm, mainly in June—August. It is not severe cold in winter and intense heat in summer, and the spring and autumn are extremely pleasant. So it is good for tourists at all seasons.

Beijing is well-known as an ancient capital for its rich historical and cultural heritage. Zhoukoudian, the "home" of Peking Man living 500,000 years ago, is located in Beijing's southwestern suburb. The history of Beijing as a city can be looked back to 3,000 years ago when it is called "Ji", the capital of the State of Yan Spring and Autumn and the Warring States Period, and the name "Yanjing" (Yan's capital) is still alive today. In the 10th century Qidan established Liao Dynasty and Beijing was the secondary capital of Liao. After the 12th century, Beijing was in succession the capitals of Jin, Yuan, Ming, and Qing Dynasties. Its history as a capital for over 800 years leaves numerous valuable historic sites and cultural relics in Beijing. At the centre of Beijing there is the Palace Museum (the Forbidden City), which is a complex of splendid and imposing ancient architecture, being the Imperial Palace in Ming and Qing Dynasties. The entire complex contains more than 9,000 various kinds of rooms covering an area of 720,000 m^2 epitomizing Chinese ancient architecture styles. This palace architecture full of oriental sentiment is very famous throughout the world. The magnificent Tian'an Men is the south gate of the Forbidden City and the grand and majestic Tian'an Men Square is in front of the gate.

The Great Wall is a spiritural emblem of the Chinese nation, while Badaling section — the most magnificent section — of the Wall is just 60 kilometer northwest of Beijing. It is the most attractive sight to tourists from China or abroad. Standing on the beacon tower of Badaling, tourists will see the Great Wall rises and falls as a huge dragon in the mountains winding its way to the horizon. Beijing also attracts worldwide attention by its beautiful imperial gardens — Summer Palace and Beihai Park — many altars, shrines, temples, taoist temples and tombs.

The old Beijing was a neatly arranged and strictly structured city spreading out from a clear axis of symmetry. Based on the old city, the new Beijing gradually expends to the all directions. Being constructed for 40 years, the present Beijing has large amount of novel modern buildings with solemn style of the old capital. It is not only well-known for its long history and rich cultural heritage, but also a functional modern city of advanced foundational facilities.

Beijing is the politics, culture and international exchange centre of the nation. There are more than 70 colleges and universities, over 500 institutions of sciences and techenologies, and numerous units and facilities for culture and sports purposes in Beijing. At the present, there are more than 140 foreign embassys, offices and UN agencies and over 70 foreign news agencies in Beijing. About 500 foreign companies set up offices in Beijing, which make up 2/3 of the registered foreign companies in China. Beijing receives thousands of delegations every year from foreign goverments, economy and trade organizations, cultural and academic groups, and people-to-people friendship associations.

Beijing is also a communication centre of China. From the grand Beijing Railway Station, trains can go directly to all the province capitals of China except Tibet, Taiwan and Hainan. Beijing International Airport is the terminal for over 40 domestic and about 20 international airlines, suppling satisfying service for tourists to Shanghai, Guanzhou, Kunming, Harbin, Xi'an, Chengdu and Urumqi in China and Karachi, Paris, Bombay, Addis Ababa, Frankfurt, London, Tokyo, San Francisco, New York, Moscow and Pyongyang abroad.

Beijing welcomes you, our friends, with good tourist services. More than 150 modern hotels, such as Beijing, Wangfu, Great Wall, Jianguo, Jinglun, Zhaolong, Xiangshan and International Hotel, are available for tourists and a large amount of taxies and bus lines extend in all directions in and out of the city.

Beijing is also famous for its supplying traditional food including Peking Duck, Mongulia "hot pot", court food and about 200 kinds of local-style snacks. Tourists will find a lot of fun in choicing in over 20,000 sorts of handicraft and souvenir in unique Beijing style.

Climate of Beijing

		Jan.	Feb.	Mar.	Apr.	May	June	July	Aug.	Sept.	Oct.	Nov.	Dec.
T (℃)	Average	−4.6	−2.1	4.7	13.0	19.9	23.6	25.8	24.4	19.1	12.2	4.3	−2.5
	Highest	10.7	15.5	22.6	31.1	36.6	38.9	39.6	38.3	32.3	29.3	23.3	13.5
	Lowest	−22.8	−17.6	−12.5	−2.4	3.7	11.2	16.1	12.3	4.9	−1.4	−11.6	−18.0
Precipitation (mm)		2.6	7.7	9.1	22.4	26.1	70.4	196.6	243.5	63.9	21.1	7.9	1.6
Wind Speed (m/s)		2.4	2.7	3.0	3.3	2.8	2.2	1.7	1.6	1.8	2.1	2.2	2.5
Seasons (Date/Month) Days		Winter 26/10−31/3 157 days			Spring 1/4−25/5 55 days		Summer 26/5−5/9 103 days			Autumn 6/9−25/10 50 days		Winter 26/10−31/3 157 days	

THE WAY TO BEIJING (AIRWAY)

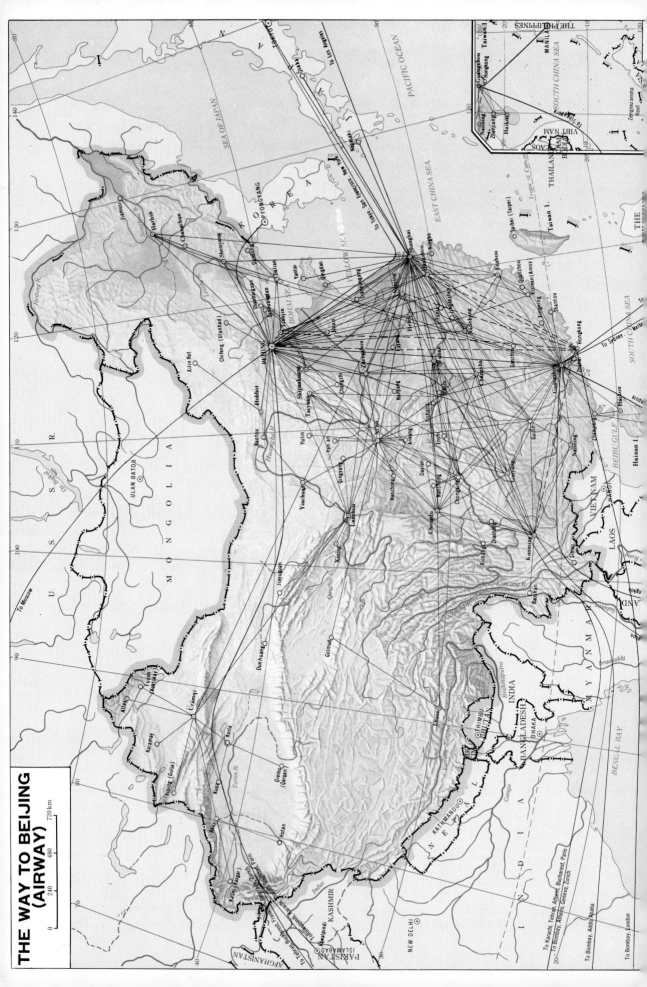

Table 1 — Beijing Booking Offices

Name	Address	Tel.
Dongsi Booking Office	117 Dongsixi Street	554515
Beitaipingzhuang Booking Office	Beisanhuanzhong Road	2015150
Zhongguancun Booking Office	Zhongguancun Road	289383
Gongzhufen Booking Office	Fuxing Avenue	266489
Hujialou Booking Office	Chaoyang Road	595613
Beijingzhan Booking Office	Beijing Railway Station	545917
Baiguanglu Booking Office	Baiguang Road	3014919
Hepingli Booking Office	Hepingli. Beijing No.171 High School	4212205

Beijing Hotel Xiyuan Hotel Holiday Inn Lido Beijing
The Great Wall Sheraton Hotel Chongwenmen Hotel
Inner Mongolia Hotel Oriental Hotel

Table 2 — Airlines

Name	Address	Tel.
Pakistan International Airline (PIA)	12-43 Diplomatic Apartments.Jianguomenwai	5323274
Air France	12-71 Diplomatic Apartments.Jianguomenwai	5323266
Philippine Airlines	12-53 Diplomatic Apartments.Jianguomenwai	5323992
Iraqi Airways	7-1-54 Diplomatic Apartments.Jianguomenwai	5321379
USSR Airlines (Aeroflot)	5-53 Diplomatic Apartments.Jianguomenwai	5323581
Swiss Air	Scite Tower.Jianguomenwai	5123555
United Airlines	Scite Tower.Jianguomenwai	5128888
British Airlines	210 Scite Tower.Jianguomenwai	512407o-210
Lufthansa German Airlines	Scite Tower.Jianguomenwai	5123500
Thai International Airways	Scite Tower.Jianguomenwai	5123881
Japan Air Lines (JAL)	Hotel Beijing-Toronto	5002221
Australia Airlines	Hotel Beijing-Toronto	5002481
Iran Airlines (IRANAIR)	Beijing International Hotel	5124940
Singapore Airlines	2 F International Manson	5004138
All Nippon Airways Co. Ltd.	2075 Beijing Hotel	5125551
Romania Airlines (Tarom)	Romania Embassy. Ritandong 'er Rd.	5323552
CAA DPRK	DPR korea Embassy. Ritandong Rd.	5323981
Cathay Pacific Airways	152 Jianguo Hotel	5003339

Table 3 — Air Routes from Beijing

Routes	Distance (km)	Days
Beijing—Shanghai	1223	1,2,3,4,5,6,7
Beijing—Tianjin	169	1,2,3,4,5,6,7
Beijing—Guangzhou	1966	1,2,3,4,5,6,7
Beijing—Hangzhou	1191	1,2,3,4,5,6,7
Beijing—Fuzhou	1796	1,2,3,4,5,6,7
Beijing—Xiamen	1791	1,2,3,4,5,6,7
Beijing—Nanjing	960	1,2,3,4,5,6,7
Beijing—Hong Kong	2152	1,2,3,4,5,6,7
Beijing—Xi'an	1039	1,2,3,4,5,6,7
Beijing—Guilin	1882	2,3,5,6,7
Beijing—Qinhuangdao	331	2,5
Beijing—Harbin	1010	1,2,3,4,5,6,7
Beijing—Changchun	925	1,2,3,4,5,6,7
Beijing—Shenyang	650	1,2,3,4,5,6,7
Beijing—Dalian	553	1,2,3,4,5,6,7
Beijing—Shijiazhuang	364	3,7
Beijing—Taiyuan	516	1,3,4,5,6
Beijing—Yan'an	822	4
Beijing—Yinchuan	982	1,5
Beijing—Zhengzhou	685	1,2,4,6
Beijing—Baotou	579	1,5
Beijing—Hohhot	435	1,2,3,4,5,6,7
Beijing—Lanzhou	1373	1,2,3,4,5,6,7
Beijing—Xining	1539	5,6
Beijing—Urumqi	2691	1,3,5,6
Beijing—Jinan	412	1,3,5,6
Beijing—Yantai	565	1,2,3,5,6
Beijing—Qingdao	636	4,6
Beijing—Lianyungang	708	6
Beijing—Hefei	954	1,4
Beijing—Wuhan	1188	1,2,3,4,5,6,7
Beijing—Changsha	1437	1,6
Beijing—Nanchang	1387	1,2,3,4,5,6,7
Beijing—Chengdu	1690	1,2,3,4,5,6,7
Beijing—Chongqing	1615	1,2,3,4,6
Beijing—Guiyang	1950	1,3,5,6
Beijing—Kunming	2215	1,2,3,5,6,7
Beijing—Nanning	2196	1,3,6
Beijing—Lhasa		6
Beijing—Haikou		1,2,6

Table 4 — Additional Air Routes

Routes	Distance (km)	Days
Beijing—Luoyang		2
Beijing—Dandong		1,3
Beijing—Qiqihar		1,3,5
Beijing—Changzhou		2,4,6
Beijing—Ningbo		2,5
Beijing—Shantou		3,4,7

Table of Railway Distances Between Major Tourist Cities (km)

	Beijing	Tianjin	Shenyang	Harbin	Dalian	Jinan	Qingdao	Nanjing	Shanghai	Hangzhou	Nanchang	Fuzhou	Zhengzhou	Wuchang	Changsha	Guangzhou	Nanning	Xi'an	Urumqi	Chengdu	Chongqing	Kunming	Taiyuan	Hohhot	Yinchuan
Beijing	Beijing																								
Tianjin	137	Tianjin																							
Shenyang	841	704	Shenyang																						
Harbin	1388	1251	547	Harbin																					
Dalian	1238	1101	397	944	Dalian																				
Jinan	494	357	1061	1608	1458	Jinan																			
Qingdao	877	750	1454	2001	1851	393	Qingdao																		
Nanjing	1157	1020	1724	2271	2121	663	1056	Nanjing																	
Shanghai	1462	1325	2029	2576	2426	968	1361	305	Shanghai																
Hangzhou	1651	1514	2218	2765	2615	1157	1550	494	189	Hangzhou															
Nanchang	2005	2142	2846	3393	3243	1793	2186	1130	825	636	Nanchang														
Fuzhou	2623	2486	3190	3737	3587	2129	2522	1466	1161	972	622	Fuzhou													
Zhengzhou	695	832	1536	2083	1933	666	1059	695	1000	1189	1310	1876	Zhengzhou												
Wuchang	1229	1366	2070	2617	2467	1200	1593	1229	1545	1356	776	1342	534	Wuchang											
Changsha	1587	1724	2428	2975	2825	1558	1951	1492	1187	998	418	984	892	358	Changsha										
Guangzhou	2313	2450	3154	3701	3551	2284	2677	2116	1811	1622	1012	1608	1618	1084	726	Guangzhou									
Nanning	2565	2702	3406	3953	3803	2536	2929	2368	2063	1874	1294	1860	1870	1336	978	1334	Nanning								
Xi'an	1165	1302	2006	2553	2403	1177	1570	1206	1511	1700	1821	2387	511	1045	1403	2129	2381	Xi'an							
Urumqi	3774	3911	4615	5162	5012	3745	4138	3774	4079	4268	4389	4955	3079	3613	3971	4697	4898	2568	Urumqi						
Chengdu	2048	2185	2889	3436	3286	2019	2412	2048	2353	2542	2236	2802	1353	1887	1920	2544	1829	842	3064	Chengdu					
Chongqing	2552	2689	3393	3940	3790	2523	2916	2552	2501	2312	1732	2298	1857	1416	1774	2040	1325	1346	3568	504	Chongqing				
Kunming	3179	3316	4020	4567	4417	3119	3512	2982	2677	2488	1908	2474	2453	1950	1592	2216	1501	1942	4164	1100	1102	Kunming			
Taiyuan	514	651	1355	1902	1752	529	922	1192	1497	1686	1953	2519	643	1177	1535	2261	2513	651	3219	1493	1997	2593	Taiyuan		
Hohhot	668	805	1509	2056	1906	1162	1555	1825	2130	2319	2673	3239	1363	1897	2255	2981	3233	1292	3037	2134	2638	3234	641	Hohhot	
Yinchuan	1346	1483	2187	2734	2584	1840	2233	2654	2813	2964	3530	3272	1143	1654	2188	2546	2359	678	1639	2143	2739	1319	678		Yinchuan

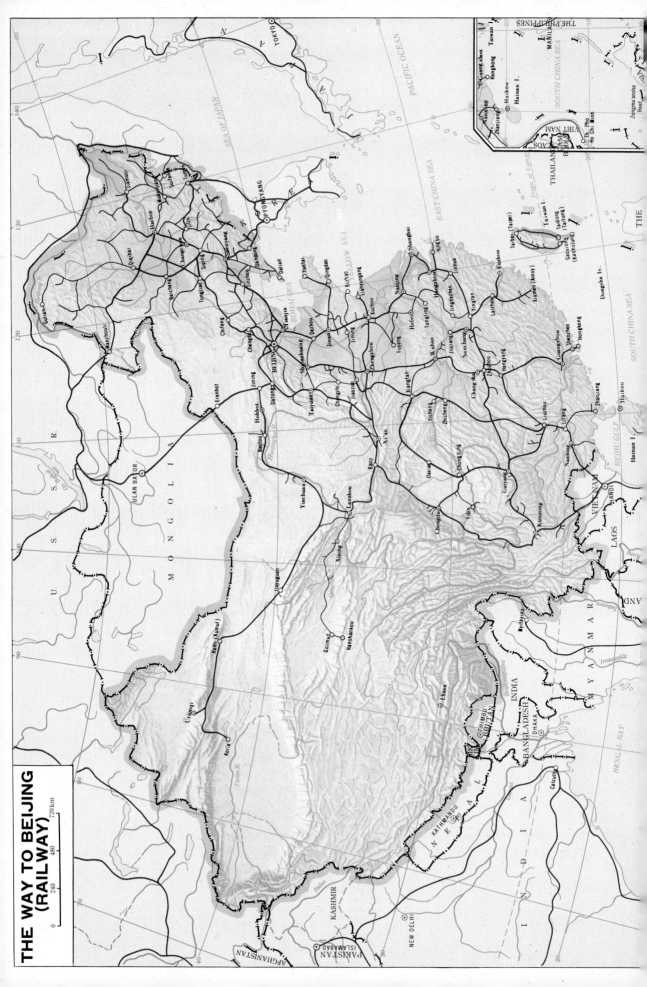

THE WAY TO BEIJING
(RAILWAY)

0   240   480   720km

Railway Booking Office

The Booking Office for Overseas Chineses and Foreign Travellers at Beijing Railway Station
Adr : 1/F 103 of VIP Waiting Room in the Station

The Booking Office of CITS Beijing Branch
Adr : 1/F Chongwenmen Hotel

The Booking Office of Beijing Overseas Chineses Travel Service
Adr : 1/F Xuanwumen Hotel

Dongdan Booking Office
Adr : West Side of Dongdanbei St.
Open-to-Booking : Beijing-Northeast China Lines , Beijing-Chengde Line
Classes of Train : Soft Sleeper , Soft Seat , Hard Sleeper , Hard Seat

Qianmen Booking Office
Adr : South of Qianmen Railway Club
Open-to-Booking : Beijing-Baotou Line , Beijing-Guangzhou Line , Lianyungang-Lanzhou Line , Shijiazhuang-Taiyuan Line
Classes of Train : Soft Sleeper , Soft Seat , Hard Sleeper , Hard Seat

Xizhimen Booking Office
Adr : In Front of Beijing North Railway Station
Open-to-Booking : Beijing-Shanghai Line , Qingdao-Jinan Line
Classes of Train : Soft Sleeper , Soft Seat , Hard Sleeper , Hard Seat (Express Trains)

Beijingjiao Booking Office
Adr : West End of 12th Lane Dongsibei St.
Open-to-Booking : All Domestic Lines
Classes of Train : Hard Seat (Express and "Slow "Trains)

Haidianlu Booking Office
Adr : At Entrace of People's Univ.
Open-to-Booking : All Domestic Lines
Classes of Train : Hard Seat (Express Train)

Beijingzhan Zhanqian Booking Office
Adr :The Front Street of Beijing Railway Station
Open-to-Booking : All Domestic Lines
Classes of Train : Hard Seat (Express Train)

Beijingzhan Booking Hall
Adr : In the Beijing Railway Station
Open-to-Booking : All Dometic Line (at that day)
Classes of Train : Soft Sleeper , Soft Seat , Hard Sleeper , Hard Seat (Express Train)

Beijingnanzhan Booking Office
Adr : In the Beijing South Railway Station
Open-to-Booking : Beijing-Harbin Line , Beijing Shanghai Line , Beijing Urbia-suburbia & Exurbia Lines
Classes of Train : Hard Sleeper , Hard Seat (Express and "Slow "Trains)

Fengtai Booking Office
Adr : Fengtai Railway Station
Open-to-Booking : Beijing-Harbin Line , Beijing Guangzhou Line-Beijing-Shanghai Line , Beijing Urbia-Suburbia & Exurbia Lines
Classes of Train : Hard Sleeper , Hard Seat (Express and "Slow "Trains)

Beijing — Harbin Line

T/No	Cl.	Dep.	Term.	Arr.
137	F.T.	8:35	Harbin	16:07
11	Exp.	6:34	Shenyang	22:23
755	Slow	6:54	Yanjiao	
165	F.T.	0:20	Mudanjiang	15:30
347	Fast	8:30	Qinhuangdao	16:43
71	Exp.	8:17	Jinan	② 10:43
167	F.T.	9:36	Nanjingxi	7:39
73	Exp.	13:10	Qingdao	② 6:25
59	Exp.	15:50	Hangzhou	② 19:08
81	Exp.	12:43	Fuzhou	③ 8:03
17	Exp.	14:30	Suzhou	③ 12:09
757	Slow	16:15	Hefei	② 12:38
27	Exp.	16:48	Shanghai	② 14:54
75	Exp.	14:50	Shanghai	② 20:52
377	Fast	17:52	Qingdao	14:20

Beijing — Shanghai Line

T/No	Cl.	Dep.	Term.	Arr.
247	F.T.	22:42	Yantai	15:30
297	F.T.	8:51	Jinan	16:43
65	Exp.	17:38	Nanjingxi	② 10:43
13	Exp.	14:40	Shanghai	7:39
239	F.T.	13:50	Qingdao	② 6:25
119	Exp.	15:23	Hangzhou	② 19:08
45	Exp.	10:38	Fuzhou	③ 8:03
109	F.T.	12:31	Suzhou	③ 12:09
127	F.T.	18:30	Hefei	② 12:38
21	Exp.	21:55	Shanghai	② 14:54
161	Exp.	21:10	Shanghai	② 20:52
25	Exp.	0:58	Qingdao	14:20

Beijing — Guangzhou Line

T/No	Cl.	Dep.	Term.	Arr.
19	Exp.	20:32	Moscow	⑦ 11:35
39	Exp.	20:32	Qiqihar	② 19:03
79	Exp.	19:40	Tianjin	21:24
289	F.T.	20:10	Jinzhou	② 5:38
253	F.T.	20:48	Shenyang	② 8:39
271	F.T.	22:07	Jilin	② 18:33
229	Exp.	23:37	Dalian	② 18:52
311	Fast	9:13	Tianjin	11:28

Beijing — Guangzhou Line

T/No	Cl.	Dep.	Term.	Arr.
1	Exp.	7:44	Changsha	② 6:00
541	Pas.	8:00	Fangshan	10:08
69	Exp.	12:58	Urumqi	④ 12:08
149	F.T.	20:00	Guiyang	③ 17:33
35	Exp.	13:30	Xi'an	10:54
389	Fast	10:18	Taiyuan	20:27
9	Exp.	9:03	Chongqing	② 17:49
245	F.T.	11:30	Wuchang	7:39
97	Exp.	11:08	Shijiazhuang	14:47
189	F.T.	17:06	Chongqing	② 7:59
373	Fast	14:12	Yuncheng	② 9:40
703	Slow	16:07	Fengtaixi	17:01
163	F.T.	8:26	Chengdu	② 21:19
37	Exp.	18:15	Wuchang	② 10:23
705	Slow	18:40	Fengtaixi	19:20
47	Exp.	19:04	Guangzhou	② 5:50
121	Exp.	21:26	Lanzhou	③ 8:22
121	Exp.	21:26	Xining	③ 13:38
279	F.T.	19:26	Xi'an	② 15:24
545	Pas.	20:21	Gaobeidian	23:04
387	Fast	21:00	Taiyuan	8:45
15	Exp.	22:30	Guangzhou	② 8:05
5	F.T.	23:27	Nanning	③ 13:40
251	F.T.	23:59	Zhengzhou	② 10:30

Beijing — Guangzhou Line

T/No	Cl.	Dep.	Term.	Arr.
61	Exp.	12:08	Kunming	③ 20:48
231	F.T.	5:54	Luoyang	19:48

Beijing — Baotou Line

T/No	Cl.	Dep.	Term.	Arr.
3	Exp.	7:40	Moscow	⑥ 11:45
323	Fast	8:50	Zhangjiakou	14:21
43	Exp.	11:01	Lanzhou	② 22:05
263	F.T.	15:10	Baotou	② 7:56
169	F.T.	17:00	Yinchuan	② 19:12
89	Exp.	18:53	Ulan Bator	② 9:55
89	Exp.	18:53	Hohhot	② 7:16
89	Exp.	18:53	Erenhot	② 10:26
295	Fast	23:21	Datong	② 6:45
295	F.T.	21:18	Baotou	② 14:01

Beijing — Chengde Line

T/No	Cl.	Dep.	Term.	Arr.
555	Pas.	6:34	Jugezhuang	9:31
91	Exp.	7:17	Chengde	11:45
551	Pas.	10:02	Chengde	17:01
557	Pas.	14:05	Jugezhuang	16:31
553	Exp.	16:29	Chengde	23:08
291	F.T.	22:18	Dadong	② 21:10

② means the Train will arrive its termination in 2nd day, others is on the analogy of this.

The Passenger Train Schedule of Arrival in Beijing

Beijing — Harbin Line

T/No	Cl.	Arr.	From	Dep.
320	Fast	21:36	Tangshan	16:38
328	Fast	12:10	Qinhuangdao	19:34

Beijing — Shanghai Line

T/No	Cl.	Arr.	From	Dep.
298	F.T.	7:10	Jinan	20:06
46	Exp.	5:45	Fuzhou	1:20
66	Exp.	15:30	Nanjingxi	8:02
14	Exp.	9:01	Shanghai	6:00
240	F.T.	11:06	Qingdao	12:00
120	F.T.	11:40	Hangzhou	18:53
128	F.T.	15:00	Hefei	9:20
22	Exp.	12:54	Shanghai	5:20
248	F.T.	16:18	Yantai	12:21
162	F.T.	18:25	Shanghai	10:38
110	F.T.	13:47	Suzhou	18:22
26	Exp.	22:50	Qingdao	16:34

Beijing — Guangzhou Line

T/No	Cl.	Arr.	From	Dep.
246	F.T.	4:00	Wuchang	17:10
122	Exp.	9:18	Lanzhou	15:24
122	Exp.	16:37	Xining	12:23
48	Exp.	10:32	Guangzhou	20:22
388	Fast	6:18	Taiyuan	17:00
252	F.T.	6:12	Zhengzhou	18:51

Beijing — Guangzhou Line

T/No	Cl.	Arr.	From	Dep.
250	F.T.	21:22	Yichang	17:20
232	F.T.	3:40	Luoyang	14:10

Beijign — Baotou Line

T/No	Cl.	Arr.	From	Dep.
90	Exp.	6:20	Ulan Bator	12:00
90	Exp.	6:20	Hohhot	17:47
90	Exp.	6:20	Erenhot	14:08
96	F.T.	7:16	Datong	23:25
264	F.T.	10:30	Baotou	18:00
170	F.T.	13:33	Yinchuan	10:40
4	Exp.	15:33	Moscow	0:30
44	Exp.	19:51	Lanzhou	8:33
324	Fast	22:40	Zhangjiakou	17:10

Beijing — Chengde Line

T/No	Cl.	Arr.	From	Dep.
554	Pas.	4:40	Chengde	21:58
556	Pas.	12:40	Jugezhuang	10:10
552	Pas.	14:00	Dandong	6:33
292	F.T.	14:52	Chengde	14:32
92	Exp.	19:41	Chengde	14:31
558	Pas.	20:29	Jugezhuang	17:41

Beijing — Harbin Line

T/No	Cl.	Arr.	From	Dep.
138	F.T.	21:45	Mudanjiang	16:38
290	F.T.	4:50	Jinzhou	19:34
60	Exp.	10:47	Changchun	20:06
20	Exp.	6:32	Moscow	1:20
40	Exp.	6:32	Qiqihar	8:02
72	Exp.	7:40	Tianjin	6:00
28	Exp.	10:00	Pyongyang	12:00
28	Exp.	9:20	Dandong	18:53
256	Slow	9:45	Shenyang	9:20
82	Exp.	5:20	Yanjiao	8:20
74	Exp.	12:21	Dalian	12:57
18	Exp.	11:55	Tianjin	10:38
230	F.T.	16:34	Sankeshu	18:22
78	F.T.	17:10	Dalian	21:00
76	Exp.	14:06	Tianjin	15:24
272	F.T.	17:30	Tianjin	12:23
80	Exp.	18:51	Jilin	20:22
758	Slow	17:40	Yanjiao	17:00
12	Exp.	20:08	Shenyang	18:51
348	Fast	21:45	Qinhuangdao	20:08
138	F.T.	4:10	Sankeshu	21:45
168	F.T.	22:28	Qiqihar	4:10
312	Fast	8:28	Tianjin	6:06

Beijing — Guangzhou Line

T/No	Cl.	Arr.	From	Dep.
544	Pas.	7:30	Fangshan	5:23
36	Exp.	11:28	Xi'an	13:46
164	F.T.	23:06	Chengdu	10:20
16	Exp.	6:00	Guangzhou	20:15
190	F.T.	8:50	Chongqing	16:24
702	Slow	9:32	Fengtaixi	8:50
6	Exp.	9:16	Nanning	18:18
98	Exp.	12:44	Shijiazhuang	9:00
38	Exp.	13:18	Wuchang	20:54
374	Fast	8:37	Yuncheng	13:20
280	F.T.	16:44	Xi'an	20:35
150	F.T.	15:55	Guiyang	18:30
62	Exp.	5:35	Kunming	21:45
704	Slow	18:06	Fengtaixi	17:24
390	Fast	18:37	Taiyuan	8:10
542	Pas.	19:14	Fangshan	17:08
146	F.T.	4:30	Nanchang	18:46
10	Exp.	20:20	Chongqing	11:11
2	Exp.	19:40	Changsha	21:20
706	Slow	21:00	Fengtaixi	20:17
70	Exp.	22:40	Urumqi	23:00
540	Pas.	22:00	Zhoukoudian	20:10
8	F.T.	17:29	Chengdu	9:16
242	F.T.	21:22	Xiangfan	23:18

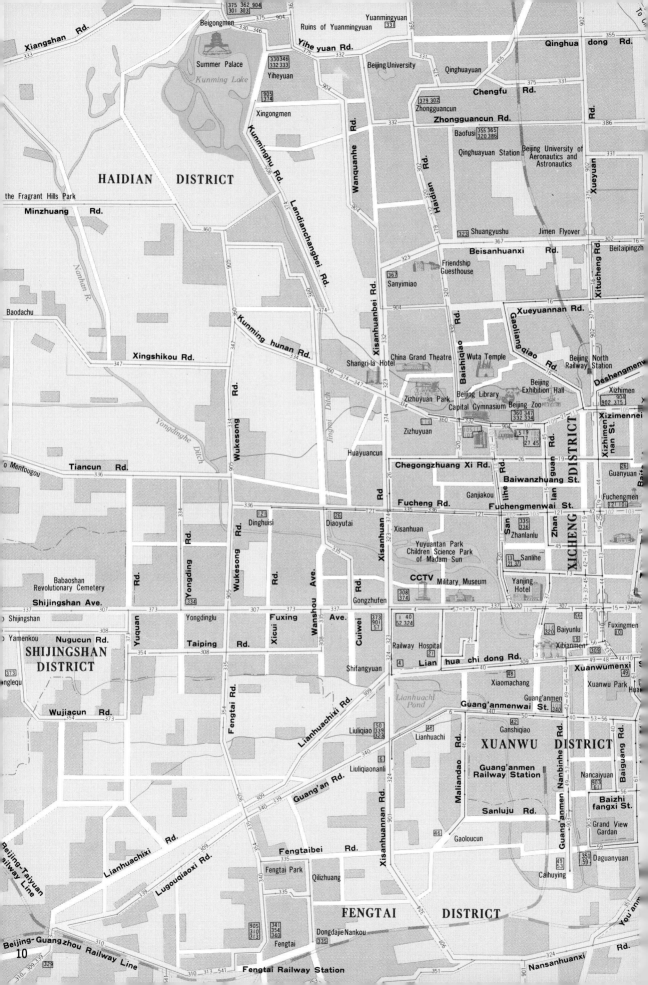

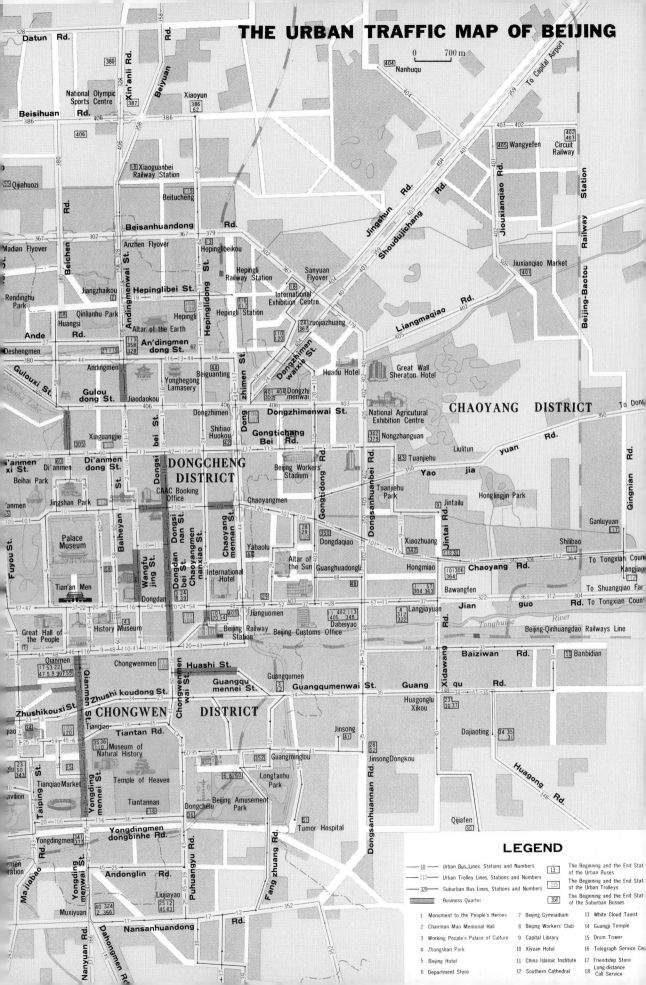

THE URBAN TRAFFIC MAP OF BEIJING

0   700 m

LEGEND

— 10 — Urban Bus Lines, Stations and Numbers
— 112 — Urban Trolley Lines, Stations and Numbers
— 328 — Suburban Bus Lines, Stations and Numbers
▨ Business Quarter

13 The Beginning and the End Stat of the Urban Buses
115 The Beginning and the End Stat of the Urban Trolleys
358 The Beginning and the End Stat of the Suburban Busses

1 Monument to the People's Heroes
2 Chairman Mao Memorial Hall
3 Working People's Palace of Culture
4 Zhongshan Park
5 Beijing Hotel
6 Department Store
7 Beijing Gymnadium
8 Beijing Workers' Club
9 Capital Library
10 Xiyuan Hotel
11 China Islamic Institute
12 Southern Cathedral
13 White Cloud Taoist
14 Guangji Temple
15 Drum Tower
16 Telegraph Service Ce
17 Friendship Store
18 Long-distance Call Service

THE SUBURBAN TRAFFIC MAP OF BEIJING

ROUTE OF BEIJING SUBWAY

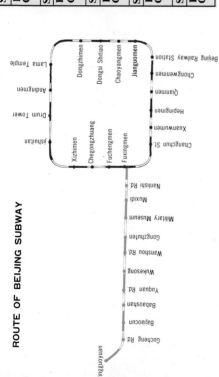

Stations: Lama Temple · Andingmen · Drum Tower · Jishuitan · Xizhimen · Chegongzhuang · Fuchengmen · Fuxingmen · Nanlishi Rd. · Muxidi · Military Museum · Gongzhufen · Wanshou Rd. · Wukesong · Yuquan Rd. · Babaoshan · Bajiaocun · Gucheng Rd. · Pingguoyuan · Dongzhimen · Dongsi Shitiao · Chaoyangmen · Jianguomen · Chongwenmen · Qianmen · Hepingmen · Xuanwumen · Changchun St. · Beijing Railway Station

Changing Buses at Stops along the Subway

Stop Name	Beijing Railway Station	Changchun St.	Wanshou Rd.	Bajiaocun	Dongsishitiao	Jishuitan
Routes of Changing Buses	9 10 20 54 103 104 48	10 25 48 38 44 45 49 309 337	308 335 373 373	337 354 325 327	117 113 115 118 44	22 27 38 44 47 331

Stop Name	Chongwenmen	Nanlishi Rd.	Wukesong	Gucheng Rd.	Dongzhimen	Xizhimen
Routes of Changing Buses	3 8 39 41 43 32 9 44 48 103 104 106 108 110 111 120	1 4 15 19 56 37 42 45 337	337 373	325 337 354 501 327 503	18 24 44 106 107 117	7 16 25 27 105 107 111 375 902

Stop Name	Qianmen	Muxidi	Yuquan Rd.	Pingguoyuan	Yonghegong	Chegongzhuang
Routes of Changing Buses	1 4 21 52 57 114 320 337	2 5 9 20 22 116 120 110 59 54 53	337 373	311 318 336 501 502	13 116	19 25 26 44

Stop Name	Hepingmen	Military Museum	Babaoshan	Jianguomen	Andingmen	Fuchengmen
Routes of Changing Buses	7 14 15 45 48 44 22	1 4 21 52 57 337	337	1 4 9 43	18 27 44 104 108 2 113 119 328 358	13 25 42 44 101 102 103

Stop Name	Xuanwumen	Gongzhufen	Chaoyangmen	Gulou	Fuxingmen
Routes of Changing Buses	15 25 48 45 22 102 105 109 307	1 4 40 52 57 308 323 324 337 373 901 374	44 101 109 110 112	27 44 58	15 25 44 56

Beijing TAXI Stations

Name	Address	Tel.
Capital TAXI Company	Beijing Hotel	513.7766 - 635
Wangfujing TAXI Company	Wangfu Hotel	512.8899 - 7509
Oriental TAXI Company	Oriental Hotel	301.4466 - 80115
	International Tennis Centre	511.2037
Jianguo TAXI	Jianguo Hotel	500.2233
Xiaoxiao TAXI Company	Beijing Roast Duck Restaurant	33.3825
Beijing TAXI Company	Beijing Railway Station · The Capital Airport	513.8833 - 4075.54.8200
	Beijing South Railway Station (Yong dingmen)·Qianmen Station	33.2543 ; 33.4981
	Fengtai Railway Station · Zhongguancun Railway Station	37.3383 ; 28.2181
	Xinjiekou Station · Xidan	66.0400 · 65.6406
	Beijing Zoo ·The Meridian Gate of Imperial Palace	89.2647 ; 55.5031 - 281
Anle TAXI Company	Xizhimen Hotel	80.2455 - 387
Huamei TAXI Company	Dongzhimen	44.7987
Shijingshan TAXI Company	Shijingshan Amusement Park	87.5170
Beijing TAXI Servie Company	6 Gongtixi Rd.	59.4040.
Beijing Long-distance Bus Company	18 Fuxingmenwai Ave.	36.6138
Guangda TAXI Company	Zizhuyuan	89.3269
Beijing Tourist-Bus Company	2 Chongwenmenxi St.	75.5126

Tourist-Bus Routes

Name	Scenic Spots	Days	Departure Time	Address of Booking Office	Tel.
Capital TAXI Company	The Great Wall (Badaling) ; Ming Tombs	1	7:00AM	Qianmen Railway Club	753775
	Fragrant Hills Park ; Summer Palace ; Temple of Azure Clouds	1	7:00AM	Northeastern Corner of Qianmen	753775
	The Great Wall ; Logging Gorge	1	7:00AM	Northwestern Corner of Chongwenmen	753775
	Chengde	3	7:00AM	Beijing Exhibition Centre	753775
	Beidaihe Beach	4	7:00AM	Qianmen Railway Club Northeastern Conner of Qianmen	753775
Beijing TAXI Company	The Great Wall ; Ming Tombs	1	6:00AM 7:00AM	Qianmenxi Street ; The Meridian Gate of Imperial Palace	7014753 553408
	Fragrant Hills ; Temple of Azure Clouds ;Temple of the Reclining Buddha	1	7:00AM	Qianmenxi Street ; The Meridian Gate of Imperial Palace	7014753 553408
	Pool and Cudrania Temple Ordination Terrace Temble	1	7:00AM	Qianmenxi Street ; The Meridian Gate of Imperial Palace	7014753 553408
	Miyun Amusement Park ; The Great Wall (Mutianyu)	1	7:00AM	Qianmenxi Street ; The Meridian Gate of Imperial Palace	7014753 553408
	The Eastern Qing Tombs	1	6:30AM	Qianmenxi Street ; The Meridian Gate of Imperial Palace	7014753 553408
	Dule Temple :Chengde Mountain Villa ; Eight Outer Temples	3	6:30AM	Qianmenxi Street ; The Meridian Gate of Imperial Palace	7014753 553408
	Beidaihe Beach ; Jiangnu Temple ; Shanhai Pass	4	6:30AM	Qianmenxi Street ; The Meridian Gate of Imperial Palace	7014753 553408
	Longqing Gorge (The Ice Lanterns Exhibition in Winter)	1	7:30AM	Qianmenxi Street ; The Meridian Gate of Imperial Palace	7014753 553408
	Beijing-Tianjin Through Line (Bus)			East End of Qianmenxi Street	654396
Long-distance Bus Company	The Great Wall ; Ming Tombs ; Ming Tombs Resrvior	1	7:00AM	Zhanlan Road	891452

& TELECOMMUNICATION FACILITIES

15

AREAS OF THE EMBASSIES OF OTHER COUNTRIES IN CHINA

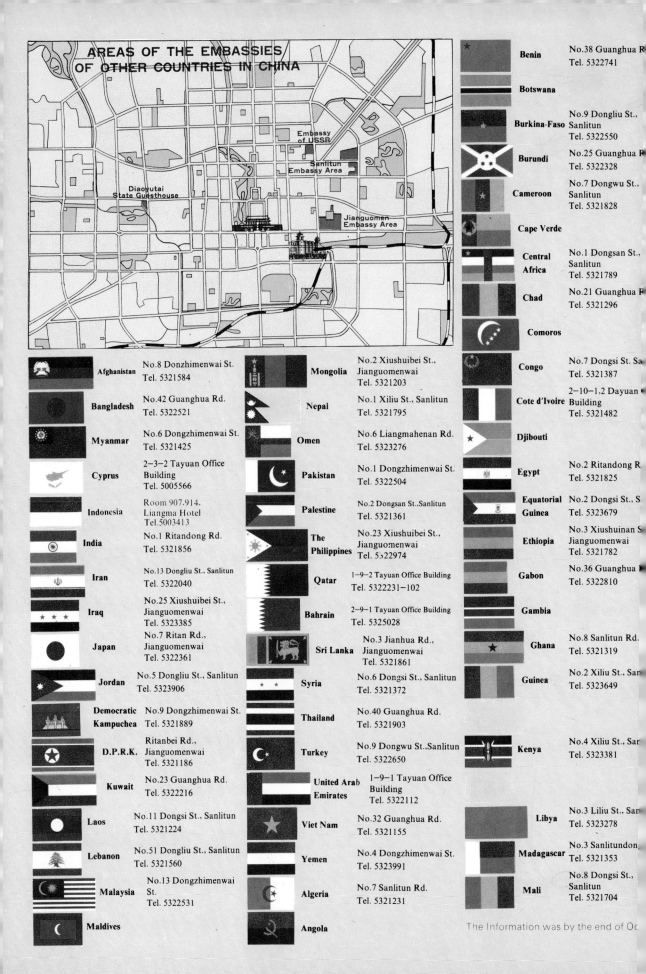

Embassy of USSR

Sanlitun Embassy Area

Diaoyutai State Guesthouse

Jianguomen Embassy Area

Afghanistan	No.8 Donzhimenwai St. Tel. 5321584
Bangladesh	No.42 Guanghua Rd. Tel. 5322521
Myanmar	No.6 Dongzhimenwai St. Tel. 5321425
Cyprus	2–3–2 Tayuan Office Building Tel. 5005566
Indonesia	Room 907.914. Liangma Hotel Tel.5003413
India	No.1 Ritandong Rd. Tel. 5321856
Iran	No.13 Dongliu St., Sanlitun Tel. 5322040
Iraq	No.25 Xiushuibei St., Jianguomenwai Tel. 5323385
Japan	No.7 Ritan Rd., Jianguomenwai Tel. 5322361
Jordan	No.5 Dongliu St., Sanlitun Tel. 5323906
Democratic Kampuchea	No.9 Dongzhimenwai St. Tel. 5321889
D.P.R.K.	Ritanbei Rd., Jianguomenwai Tel. 5321186
Kuwait	No.23 Guanghua Rd. Tel. 5322216
Laos	No.11 Dongsi St., Sanlitun Tel. 5321224
Lebanon	No.51 Dongliu St., Sanlitun Tel. 5321560
Malaysia	No.13 Dongzhimenwai St. Tel. 5322531
Maldives	

Mongolia	No.2 Xiushuibei St., Jianguomenwai Tel. 5321203
Nepal	No.1 Xiliu St., Sanlitun Tel. 5321795
Omen	No.6 Liangmahenan Rd. Tel. 5323276
Pakistan	No.1 Dongzhimenwai St. Tel. 5322504
Palestine	No.2 Dongsan St.,Sanlitun Tel. 5321361
The Philippines	No.23 Xiushuibei St., Jianguomenwai Tel. 5322974
Qatar	1–9–2 Tayuan Office Building Tel. 5322231–102
Bahrain	2–9–1 Tayuan Office Building Tel. 5325028
Sri Lanka	No.3 Jianhua Rd., Jianguomenwai Tel. 5321861
Syria	No.6 Dongsi St., Sanlitun Tel. 5321372
Thailand	No.40 Guanghua Rd. Tel. 5321903
Turkey	No.9 Dongwu St.,Sanlitun Tel. 5322650
United Arab Emirates	1–9–1 Tayuan Office Building Tel. 5322112
Viet Nam	No.32 Guanghua Rd. Tel. 5321155
Yemen	No.4 Dongzhimenwai St. Tel. 5323991
Algeria	No.7 Sanlitun Rd. Tel. 5321231
Angola	

Benin	No.38 Guanghua R Tel. 5322741
Botswana	
Burkina-Faso	No.9 Dongliu St., Sanlitun Tel. 5322550
Burundi	No.25 Guanghua R Tel. 5322328
Cameroon	No.7 Dongwu St., Sanlitun Tel. 5321828
Cape Verde	
Central Africa	No.1 Dongsan St., Sanlitun Tel. 5321789
Chad	No.21 Guanghua F Tel. 5321296
Comoros	
Congo	No.7 Dongsi St. Sa Tel. 5321387
Cote d'Ivoire	2–10–1,2 Dayuan Building Tel. 5321482
Djibouti	
Egypt	No.2 Ritandong R Tel. 5321825
Equatorial Guinea	No.2 Dongsi St., S Tel. 5323679
Ethiopia	No.3 Xiushuinan S Jianguomenwai Tel. 5321782
Gabon	No.36 Guanghua F Tel. 5322810
Gambia	
Ghana	No.8 Sanlitun Rd. Tel. 5321319
Guinea	No.2 Xiliu St., San Tel. 5323649
Kenya	No.4 Xiliu St., San Tel. 5323381
Libya	No.3 Liliu St., San Tel. 5323278
Madagascar	No.3 Sanlitundon, Tel. 5321353
Mali	No.8 Dongsi St., Sanlitun Tel. 5321704

Mauritania	No.9 Dongsan St., Sanlitun Tel. 5321346	Denmark	No.1 Dongwu St., Sanlitun Tel. 5322431	Bolivia	3-1-142 Tayuan Office Building Tel. 5324370
Mauritius		Finland	1-10-1 Tayuan Office Building Tel. 5321817	Brazil	No.27 Guanghua Rd. Tel. 5322881
Morocco	No.16 Sanlitun Rd. Tel. 5321796	France	No.3 Dongsan St.,Sanlitun Tel. 5321331	Canada	No.10 Sanlitun Rd. Tel. 5323536
Mozambique	1-7-1 Tayuan Office Building Tel. 5323664	Germany, Federal Republic	No.5 Dongzhimenwai St. Tel. 5322161	Chile	No.1 Dongsi St., Sanlitun Tel. 5322074
Niger	No.11 Dongliu St.,Sanlitun Tel. 5322768			Colombia	No.34 Guanghua Rd. Tel. 5323377
Nigeria	No.2 Dongwu St., Sanlitun Tel. 5323631	Greece	No.19 Guanghua Rd. Tel. 5321317	Cuba	No.1 Xiushinan St., Jianguomenwai Tel. 5322822
Rwanda	No.30 Xiushuibei St., Jianguomenwai Tel. 5322193	Hungary	No.10 Dongzhimenwai St. Tel. 5321431	Ecuador	11-21 Jianguomenwai Office Building Tel. 5322158
Sao Tome and Principe		Iceland		Guyana	No.1 Xiushuidong St., Jianguomenwai Tel. 5321337
Senegal	No.1 Ritandongyi St., Jianguomenwai Tel. 5322593	Ireland	No.3 Ritandong Rd. Tel. 5322691	Jamaica	
Seychelles		Italy	No.2 Dong'er St., Sanlitun Tel. 5323114	Mexico	No.5 Dongwu St., Sanlitun Tel. 5322122
Sierra Leone	No.7 Dongzhimenwai St. Tel. 5321446	Luxembourg	No.21 Neiwubu St. Tel. 556175	Nicaragua	2-12-2 Tayuan Office Building Tel. 5323014
Somalia	No.2 Sanlitun Rd. Tel. 5321752	Malta	2-1-22 Tayuan Office Building Tel. 5323114	Peru	2-82 Sanlitun Office Building Tel. 5324658
Sudan	No.1 Dong'er St., Sanlitun Tel. 5323715	The Netherlands	1-15-2,2-15-1,2 Tayuan Office Building Tel. 5321131	Suriname	
Tanzania	No.53 Dongliu St., Sanlitun Tel. 5321491	Norway	No.1 Dongyi St., Sanlitun Tel. 5322261	Trinidad and Tobago	
Togo	No.11 Dongzhimenwai St. Tel. 5322202	Poland	No.1 Ritan Rd., Jianguomenwai Tel. 5321235	U.S.A.	No.3 Xiushuibei St., Jianguomenwai Tel. 5323831
Tunisia	No.1 Sanlitundong St. Tel. 5322435	Portugal	2-72 Sanlitun Office Building Tel. 5323497	Uruguay	2-7-2 Tayuan Office Building Tel. 5324445
Uganda	No.5 Sanlitundong St. Tel. 5321708	Romania	Ritanludong'er St. Tel. 5323315	Venezuela	No.14 Sanlitun Rd. Tel. 5321295
Zaire	No.6 Dongwu St., Sanlitun Tel. 5321995	San Marino		Australia	No.15 Dongzhimenwai St. Tel. 5322331
Zambia	No.5 Dongsi St., Sanlitun Tel. 5321554	Spain	No.9 Sanlitun Rd. Tel. 5323629	Fiji	
Zimbabwe	No.7 Dongsan St., Sanlitun Tel. 5323795	Sweden	No.3 Dongzhimenwai St. Tel. 5323331	Kiribati	
Albania	No.28 Guanghua Rd. Tel. 5321120	Switzerland	No.3 Dongwu St., Sanlitun Tel. 5322736	New Zealand	No.1 Ritanludong'er St. Tel. 5322731
Austria	No.5 Xiushuinan St., Jianguomenwai Tel. 5322061	U.S.S.R.	No.4 Dongzhimenbeizhong St. Tel. 5322051	Papua New Guiner	2-11-2 Tayuan Office Building Tel. 5324312
Belgium	No.6 Sanlitun Rd. Tel. 5321736	Yugoslavia	No.1 Dongliu St.,Sanlitun Tel. 5323516	New Caiedonia	
United Kingdom	No.11 Guanghua Rd. Tel. 5321961	Antigua and Barbuda		Western Samoa	
Bulgaria	No.4 Xiushuibei St., Jianguomenwai Tel. 5321179	Argentina	No.11 Dongwu St., Sanlitun Tel. 5322090	Singapore	No.4 Liangmahenan Rd. Tel. 5323926
Czechoslovakia	Ritan Rd.,Jianguomenwai Tel. 5321531	Barbados		Saudi Arabia	7-2-41 Tayuan Office Building Tel. 5324825

Beijing Newly-Selected Sixteen Scenes

On Oct.9,1988, " Beijing Newly–Selected Sixteen Scenes" was chosen through a public appraisal sponsored by over 60 institutions in Beijing. They are Tian'anmen Square, the Palace Museum, the Great Wall at Badaling, Beihai Park, the Summer Palace, the Temple of Heaven, Fragrant Hills, Ten Ferries, Zhoukoudian Site of Peking Man, Longqing Gorge, the Great Bell Temple, White Dragon's Pool, the Ming Tombs, Lugouqiao (Marco Polo) Bridge, the Great Wall at Mutianyu, and Grand View Garden.

The Best Sightseeing Lines In Beijing

There are numerous places of historic interest and scenic beauty in Beijing. Besides the Beijing Newly–Selected 16 Scenes, Beijing Zoo, Jingshan Park, Yonghegong Lamasery (the Lama Temple), the Ruins of Yuanmingyuan, the Temple of Azure Clouds, the Temple of the Reclining Buddha, Eight Scenic Spots of Western Mountains, the Pool and Cudrania Temple, Ordination Terrace Temple and Stone–Flower Cave are also included in this atlas. If tourists have less time and want to see more in Beijing, a proper management should be made to save the money and time. Here we offer you seven One–day Touring Lines which can meet your need.

First Day: Tian'anmen Square, Palace Museum, Jingshan Park and Beihai Park in the urban district

The Tian'anmen Square is the largest square in the world. After watching the flag–rising ceremony in the early morning, you may visit some magnificent buidings such as the Rostrum of Tian'anmen, the Monument of the People's Heroes, Chairman Mao Memorial Hall, the Great Hall of the People, the Museum of Chinese Revolution History, and Zhengyang Gate.

Passing through Tian'anmen, Duanmen Gate and Meridian Gate, now you are in the largest imperial palace extant in the world — the Palace Museum. Opposite the rare gate of the palace, Gate of Military Prowess, is the Jingshan Park, and not far from the west side of the Jingshan Park is the Beihai Park, which is the most completely preserved ancient garden in China.

Second Day: the Summer Palace, Fragrant Hills Park, the Temple of Azure Clouds, the Temple of the Reclining Buddha and Cao Xueqin's Former residence in the suburbs

Take Bus Lines 332,374 or 375 to the Summer Palace, then 333 to the Temple of Reclining Buddha, Cao Xueqin's Former Residence, the Temple of Azure Clouds and Fragrant Hills. Autumn in the best season for tourists to visit the Fragrant Hills, when tourists may enjoy the red autumnal leaves all over the hills. Taking Bus Lines 360 or 318 and then the subway, people can go from the Fragrant Hills to the city. Of course, there are also several Express Lines for tourists service between the city and the Summer Palace, the Temple of Reclining Buddha, the Temple of Azure Clouds and Fragrant Hills.

Third Day: the Great Wall at Badaling, Changling Tomb, the Underground Palace of Dingling Tomb and the Ming Tombs Reservior in the outer suburbs

Tourists can take Express Line to the Great Wall at Badaling, the Underground Palace of Dingling Tomb and the Ming Tombs Reservior, etc., or take train No. 577 or 579 from Xizhimen Railway Station (Beijing North Station) to the Great Wall at Badaling, and come back to the city by train No.578 or 580 in the afternoon. Another choice is to take Bus Line 345 from Deshengmen to Changping, and then Line 314 to the Underground Palace of the Ming Tombs.

Fourth Day: the Grand View Garden and the Temple of Heaven

Take Bus Line 59 to the Grand View Garden in the morning, and on the way back in the afternoon, drop at Tianqiao Station to visit the Temple of Heaven.

Fifth Day: Ordination Terrace Temple and the Pool and Cudrania Temple

By subway to Pingguoyuan, then Bus Line 326 to Hetan, and then the Express Bus Line. tourists can reach Ordination Terrace Temple and Pool and Cudrania Temple. Bus Line 336 at Zhanlanlu Road also go to Hetan.

Sixth Day: Zhoukoudian Site of Peking Man and Lugou (Marco Polo) Bridge

There is a Long–distance Bus Line at Tianqiao to the Zhoukoudian Site of Peking Man. In the afternoon, on the way back to the city, you may drop at Lugou Bridge and pay a visit there.

Seventh Day: Yonghegong Lamasery (the Lama Temple) and Beijing Zoo

Tourists can take Bus Lines 13 or 116, or subway, to Yonghegong Lamasery in the morning, then, in the afternoon, take Bus Line 44 or subway to Xizhimen, and then transfer to Bus Lines 7,105,107 or 111 to Beijing Zoo.

There are also Express Bus Lines from Beijing City to the Eastern Qing Tombs in Zunhua County, the Western Qing Tombs in Yixian County, Chengde Summer Resort and Beidaihe Coast.

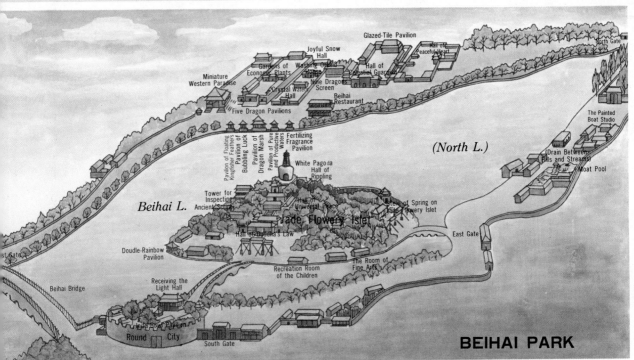

Labels on the map:

Glazed-Tile Pavilion · Hall of Peaceful Heart · North Gate · Joyful Snow Hall · Washing Orchid House · Gardens of Economic Plants · Hall of Celestial Guardian · Miniature Western Paradise · Crystal Water Hall · Nine Dragons Screen · Beihai Restaurant · Five Dragon Pavilions · The Painted Boat Studio · Pavilion of Floating Kingfisher Feathers · Pavilion of Bubbling Luck · Pavilion of Dragon Marsh · Pavilion of Pure and Productive Waters · Fertilizing Fragrance Pavilion · (North L.) · (Drain Between Halls and Streams) · Moat Pool · White Pagoda · Hall of Rippling · Tower for Inspecting Ancient Script · Beihai L. · Hall of Universal Peace · Jade Flowery Islet · Hall of Spring on Jade Flowery Islet · East Gate · Hall of Buddha's Law · Doudle-Rainbow Pavilion · Recreation Room of the Children · The Room of Fine Arts · West Gate · Beihai Bridge · Receiving the Light Hall · Jade Bowl Pavilion · Round City · South Gate

BEIHAI PARK

ine-Dragon Screen

The park was originally a palace constructed by Liao emperors in the 10th century for short stays away from the capital. During the Jin, Yuan, Ming and Qing times, it was an imperial garden. Covering an area of more than 700,000m^2, half of which is occupied by waters, it is famous for the beautiful hill in the middle of water — the Jade Flowery Islet — clear water of Beihai, which is in fact a man-dug lake, and White Dagoba. Legend has it that the Jade Flowery Islet, located at the park's center, was built in the style of the fairy mountain believed in ancient times to exist somewhere in the East Sea. On this islet towers the White Dagoba, and among the luxuriant growth of verdant pines and cypresses stand halls and pavilions such as the Temple of Long Peace (Yong'ansi), the waterside long corridor and the Rippling Hall (Yilantang) which were built in imitation of the Gold Mountain Temple (Jinshansi). Other scenic spots in the park include the Hall of Peaceful Heart (Jingxinzhai), the Moat Pool (Haopujian), the Painted Boat Studio (Huafangzhai), the Five-Dragon Pavilion (Wulonting), the Nine-Dragon Screen (Jiulongbi) and the Round City, where many cultural relics (jade Buddhist statue, jade vat, etc.) are kept.

THE IMAGE MAP OF TIANANMEN SQUARE, IMPERIAL PALACE AND JINGSHAN PARK

Palace Moat

Palace Moat

Palace Moat

Imperial Longevity Hall

Chiban Longevity Hall

Gate of Divine Military Genius

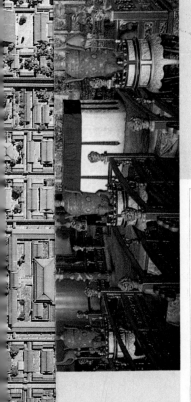

gods. The imperial garden boasts a typical royal style with its ingenious lay-out; the eastern halls are now used for displaying antiques including pottery and porcelain wares, bronze objects, paintings and precious articles of art; the western halls are used for showing reconstructions of the former rooms.

Tian'anmen Square

The square which lies at the center of urban Beijing was formerly an imperial square in front of the Forbidden City. Large-scale expansion after 1949 has turned it into the biggest square in the famous cities of the world, covering an area of 440,000 m² and capable of accomodating an assembly of one million people. North of the square stands Tian'anmen (Gate of Heavenly Peace), the main gate of the Forbidden City of the Ming and Qing Dynasties, where imperial decrees were promulgated. Sitting on the top of the gate is a tall tower, which looks extremely magnificent, with white marble bridges spanning the moat (the Gold-water River) below, and carved stone ornamental columns (Huabiao), stone lions and newly built flower beds standing in the front. The Gate of Heavenly Peace is closely related to many important historical events of the country such as the May—4th Patriotic Movement and the founding ceremony of New China; it is therefore referred to as the symbol of New China and held in respect by the Chinese people. This is why the gate, with its historical significance and architectural magnificence, is attracting visitors

---

PALACE MUSEUM

Palace Moat

0   64 m   *Palace Moat*

Turret
Turret

Palace of Longevity and Peace
Spring Happiness Hall
Heroic Splendour Hall

Palace of Mighty Glory
Hall of Devoted Esteem (Honour)
Full Happiness Palace
Empress Assistant Palace
Basis Propety Hall
Pavilion of Rain Flower

Divine Military Genius
Gate of Military Genius
Chastise Obedience Gate
Imperial Peace Hall
Imperial Garden
Concentrated Elegance Palace
Earthly Tranquility Gate
Earthly Peace Gate
Hall of Vigorous Fertility
Palace of Eternal Longevity
Flowery Moon Gate
Heavenly Purity Palace
Heavenly Purity Gate

Chastise Obedience Gate
Respect Auspiciousness Pavilion
Combined Harmony Porch
Happiness Longevity Hall
Diligent Hall
Character Cultivation Hall
Character Cultivation Gate
Peaceful Longevity Palace
Imperial Supremacy Hall
Gate of Peaceful Longevity
Gate of Imperial Supremacy
Nine-Dragon Screen

North-Five Abodes
Southern View Palace
Eternal Harmony Palace
Prolonged Happiness Palace

Palace in Honour Worshipping Ancestors
Hall of Worshipping Ancestors
Gate of Worshipping Ancestors

Solar Essence Gate

Gate of Group of the South Houses
Respect Movement South Houses
Gate of Peace Celebration

Imperial Kitchen and Tea House
South Three Abodes

Archery Pavilion
Lofty Tower

...um of Art Works ...h the Dynasties

Preserving Harmony Hall
Complete Harmony Hall

West three Abodes
Real Hall of Magnificent Buddha
Palace of Peace and Tranquility
Vigorous Old Age Hall
Peace Tranquility Gate
Hall of the Culture of the Mind
Solemn Ancestor Gate
Lofty Tower

...um of Art Works ...gh the Dynasties

Tender Shade Tower
Unification House
Tender Tranquility Garden
Bordering Confronted the Stream Pavilion

both at home and from abroad.

Towering on the square is the Monument to the People's Heroes and on the four sides of the monument are relief sculptures depicting the various scenes of the revolution of the Chinese people. In the due south of the square, just inside Zhengyangmen (the Gate of the Rising Sun) stands the majestic Memorial Hall to Chairman Mao, in which there are rooms devoted to the memory of the revolutionary deeds of Mao Zedong, Liu Shaoqi, Zhou Enlai and Zhu De. Flanking the square are the Museum of the Chinese History and the Museum of the Chinese Revolution on the east side, and the Great Hall of the People on the west side. The three of them are among the ten major buildings put up in the 1950s. The Great Hall of the People is the meeting place of the National Peoples' Congress; it has halls which are furnished in different styles of China's various provinces and regions.

Northwest of the square is the Zhongshan Park (Dr. Sun Yat-sen Park). In the park is the altar where the Ming and Qing emperors offered sacrifices to the God of Land and the God of Grains. The altar is filled with earth in five different colours, with yellow earth placed in the middle, signifying that "all land under the sun belongs to the emperor". Northeast of the square is the Cultural Palace of the Labouring People, which used to be the ancestral temple of the Ming and Qing rulers but is now a place of relaxation and cultural activities for the people.

Fig.1   Jingshan Park

Fig.2   Overlooking the Imperial Palace

Fig.3   Throne for Emperor

Fig.4   The Festival Night in Tian'anmen Square

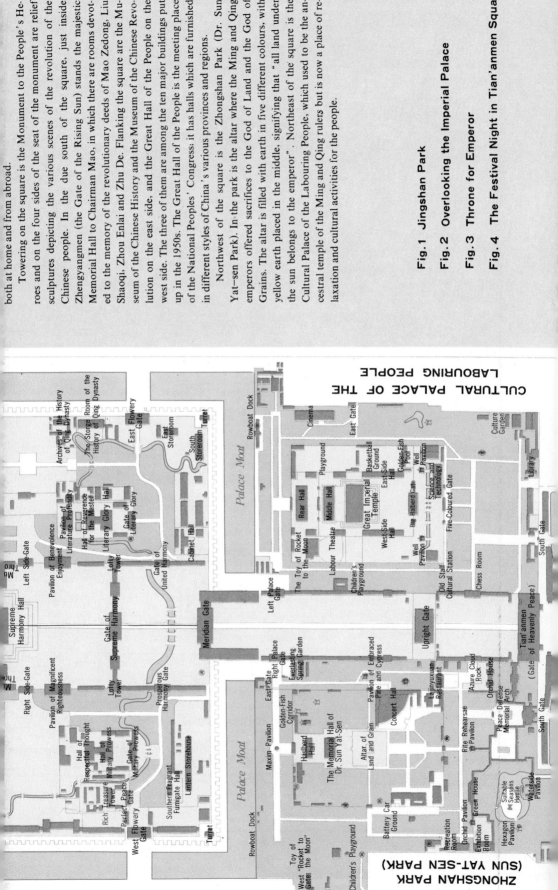

North Eighth To

North Fourth Tower

Battery

The Industrial and commercial
Administrative Office

Yanshan Restaurant
Reclining Dragon
Restaurant   Lock and key
                Shop   of North Gate
South Fourth Tower
          Shop   Foreign Guest Restaurant
          Parking Lot

      Restaurant   Shop
                                    Outer Town of
                                    Juyong Pass

                                              Statue of Dr. Zhan Tia

                                                              Juy

Qinglongqiao New   Qinglongqiao
Railway Station   Blue-Dragon-Bridge   Railway Station

0   140m

The Great Wall at Badaling

The Great Wall is one of the architectural wonders of the world, a triumph of engineering which has in the course of time won the name "a spectacle of the universe". It was first built about 2500 years ago, during the Warring States period, and then extended and fortified in the subsequent dynasties — the Qin, Han and Ming. Typicality of the Great Wall is the section at Badaling, a strategically important point and a hub of communication in the mountainous region north of Beijing since ancient times. This section, once a component part of the northern defence system of the Ming Dynasty, winds its way like a flying dragon among the steep mountains outside the Juyong Pass, having a height of 6—7m, and a width great enough for five horses to march abreast. There is a museum at this section now. The Juyong Pass was listed as one of the scenery highlights in the area of the ancient capital for its rolling green hills. Scenic spots near the pass are Guancheng of the Ming Dynasty and Yuntai of the Yuan Dynasty, which are well known for their stone carvings.

Fig.1 The Great Wall at Badaling

Fig.2 Juyong Pass

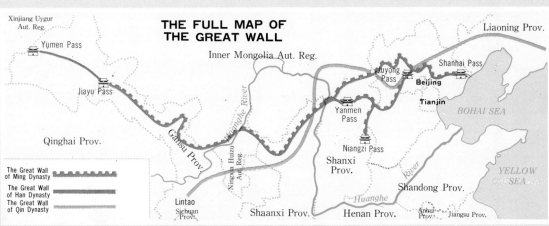

THE FULL MAP OF
THE GREAT WALL

Xinjiang Uygur Aut. Reg.

Yumen Pass

Inner Mongolia Aut. Reg.

Liaoning Prov.

Juyong Pass

Shanhai Pass

Beijing

Jiayu Pass

Huanghe River

Tianjin

BOHAI SEA

Qinghai Prov.

Gansu Prov.

Ningxia Huizu Aut. Reg.

Yanmen Pass

Niangzi Pass

Shanxi Prov.

Shandong Prov.

YELLOW SEA

The Great Wall of Ming Dynasty

The Great Wall of Han Dynasty

The Great Wall of Qin Dynasty

Lintao

Sichuan Prov.

Shaanxi Prov.

Huanghe

Henan Prov.

Anhui Prov.

Jiangsu Prov.

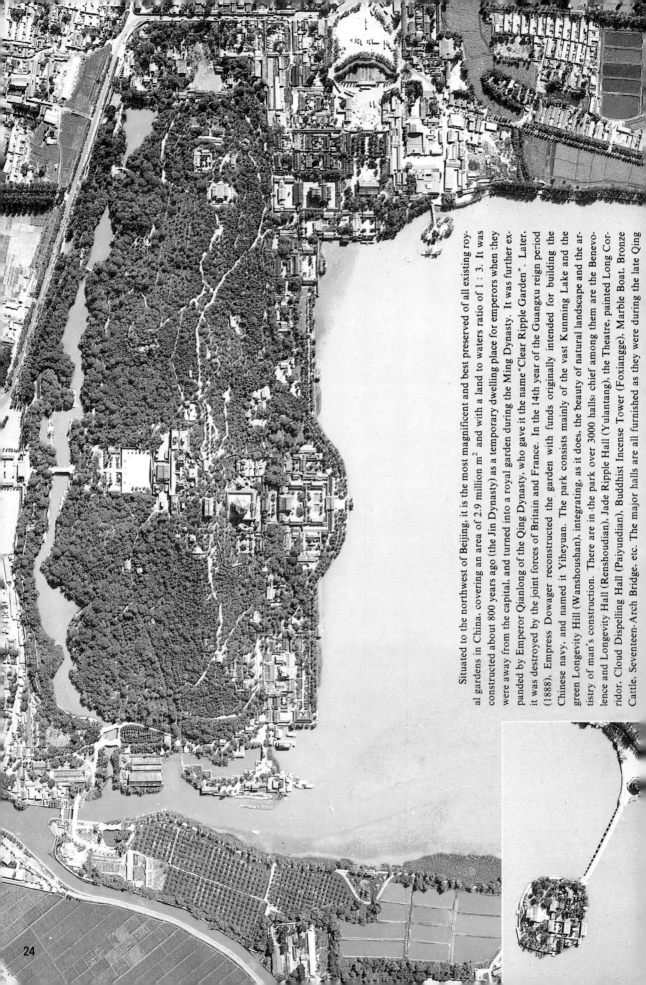

Situated to the northwest of Beijing, it is the most magnificent and best preserved of all existing royal gardens in China, covering an area of 2.9 million m² and with a land to waters ratio of 1 : 3. It was constructed about 800 years ago (the Jin Dynasty) as a temporary dwelling place for emperors when they were away from the capital, and turned into a royal garden during the Ming Dynasty. It was further expanded by Emperor Qianlong of the Qing Dynasty, who gave it the name "Clear Ripple Garden". Later, it was destroyed by the joint forces of Britain and France. In the 14th year of the Guangxu reign period (1888), Empress Dowager reconstructed the garden with funds originally intended for building the Chinese navy, and named it Yiheyuan. The park consists mainly of the vast Kunming Lake and the green Longevity Hill (Wanshoushan), integrating, as it does, the beauty of natural landscape and the artistry of man's construction. There are in the park over 3000 halls; chief among them are the Benevolence and Longevity Hall (Renshoudian), Jade Ripple Hall (Yulantang), the Theatre, painted Long Corridor, Cloud Dispelling Hall (Paiyundian), Buddhist Incense Tower (Foxiangge), Marble Boat, Bronze Cattle, Seventeen-Arch Bridge, etc. The major halls are all furnished as they were during the late Qing

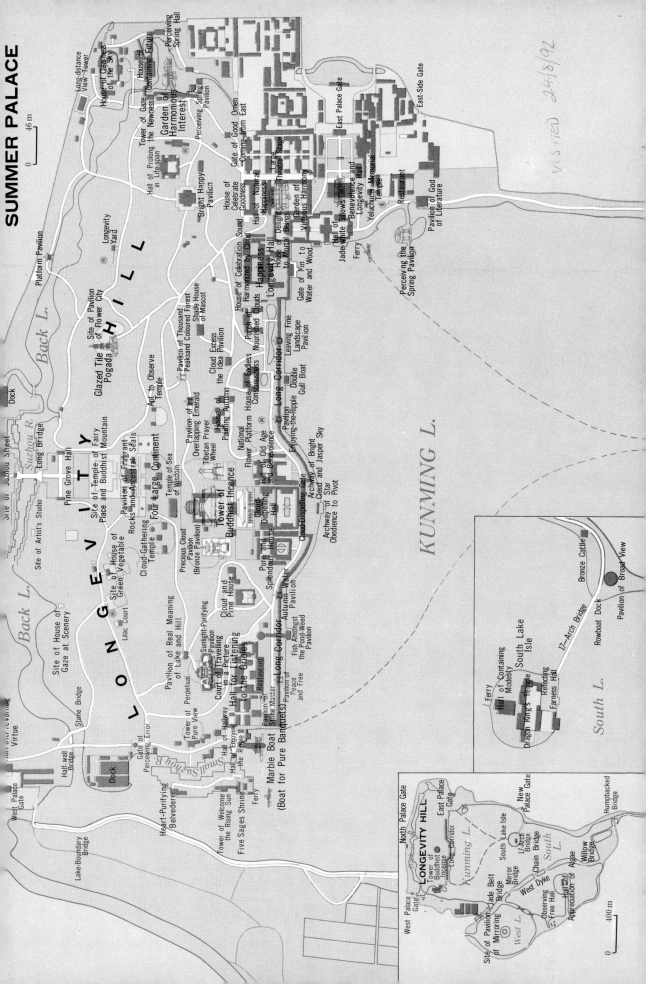

Upper Station
The Incense Burner Peak

Middle Station

Stele of Western Hills
Shimmering in Snow

Platform

Forest of Red Autumnal Leaves

Cable Car

Villa of Clambing to Cloud

Villa of Moon Perch

Pavilion of Various Scenery

Fourth Court of Jade Flower

Pavilion of Spacious Wind

Jade Splendour
Mountain Villa

Dome of Jade Fragrance

Pavilion of
White Bark Pine

Villa of Jade Flower

Avalokitesvara Pavilion

Diamond Throne Pagoda

Temple of Bright Glow

The Mid Mountain Pavilion

Glazed Tile Pagoda

Argats Hall   Sun Yat-sen Memorial

Luminous Temple

Heart-Seeing Study

Restaurant of A?

The Ruins of
The Fragrant Hill Temple

Cloudy Pavilion

Rest of Pilgrim

Double Clarity

Rising Cloud

Pavilion of
Viewing Peak

Spectacles
Lake Low Station

North Gate

Hotel of Fragrant Hill

Lake of Steady
Green Jade

Administrative Office   Villa of Fragrant Hills

East Gate

0   75m

Fragrant Hills Park

Situated at the foot of the Incense Burner Peak (Xianglufeng) northwest of Beijing, the park boasts a long history and is famous for its wooded mountains. During the Jin, Yuan, Ming and Qing times, all the emperors put up villas here, making it a place for relaxation and pleasure-seeking. It reached the peak of prosperity during the reign period of Emperor Qianlong of the Qing Dynasty, when it was called the Garden of Tranquility and Charm (Jingyiyuan). Covering an area of 1,500,000 m², the park has many scenic spots. In the north, there are the Tibetan-style Temple — the Luminous Temple (Zhaomiao) — the glazed pagoda with seven tiers of eaves and the Heart-Seeing Study (Jianxinzhai); in the middle part of the park there are the Jade Splendour Mountain Villa (Yuhua-

shanzhuang) surrounded by soaring ancient trees and one of the eight scenery highlights of Yanjing, the ancient capital, known as White Snow Under the Sun at the Western Hills; in the south, there are the steep Mountain of Jade Hand Tablet (Senyuhu), the ruins of Fragrant Hills Temple (Xiangshansi), the place where the Central Committee of the Communist Party of China stayed on the eve of the founding of the People's Republic of China, and the Double Clarity villa (Shuangqingbieshu), which is referred to as a garden within the garden. The park is indeed a place "where people can enjoy flowers in spring, escape from the heat in summer, view red leaves in autumn and go for a walk on the snow-covered ground in winter".

Temple of Azure Clouds

Located north of the Fragrant Hills Park, it is the most magnificent ancient temple in the area of Western Hills. It was constructed in the 26th year in the Zhiyuan reign period of the Yuan Dynasty (1289). A hall housing 508 arhats was put up in imitation of Jingci Temple of Hangzhou during the reign of Qianlong of the Qing Dynasty, and a pagoda was constructed on the hill at the rear, too. With these additions, the temple became a place frequented by the royalty. It consists of six courtyards, which are laid out on six progressively higher levels along the mountain slope in a secluded environment. The 508 arhats, each having a different facial expression and posture, are precious works of art. When Dr. Sun Yat-sen passed away in 1925, his coffin was placed in this temple. When his remains were removed to Nanjing for burial in 1929, his hat and clothing were kept in the pagoda at the rear hill. There is hall here devoted to his memory.

The Temple of Azure Clouds

The Hall of Arhats

Red-leaves in the Fragrant Hills Park

27

Overlooking the Temple of Heaven

VISITED 23/8/92

The Hall of Prayer for Good Harvests

Situated in the southern suburbs of Beijing, the park used to be the place where emperors of the Ming and Qing Dynasties offered sacrifices to heaven, praying for bumper harvests. It is the largest existing architectural complex for imperial sacrificial ceremonies in China, covering an area of 2.7 million m^2. The complex consists of the Hall of Prayer for Good Harvests (Qiniandian), the Circular Altar and the Abstinence Hall (Zhaigong). The Hall of Prayer for Good Harvests, 38m tall, cone-shaped and with three tiers of eaves, is supported by pillars standing in three rings — the inner, middle and outer rings — representing respectively the four seasons, the twelve months and the twelve two-hour periods. At the southern end of the God's path in front of the hall stands the Circular Altar, where the sacrificial ceremony was held, and the Echo Wall, which added greatly to the mystery of the altar, suggesting that a dialogue was going on between the emperor and the heaven.

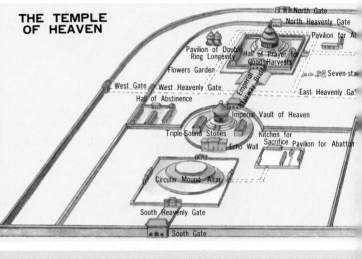

THE TEMPLE OF HEAVEN

North Gate

North Heavenly Gate

Pavilion for A...

Pavilion of Double Ring Longevity

Hall of Prayer for Good Harvests

Flowers Garden

Seven-sta...

West Gate   West Heavenly Gate

Emperial Stairway Bridge

East Heavenly Ga...

Hall of Abstinence

Imperial Vault of Heaven

Triple-Sound Stones

Kitchen for Sacrifice   Pavilion for Abattoir

Echo Wall

Circular Mound Altar

South Heavenly Gate

South Gate

Ten Ferries

These ferries are located in the middle and upper reaches of the Juma River, over 100km to the southwest of Beijing, in an area through which the railway leading to Yuanping, Shanxi Province passes. As there are altogether ten of them, hence the name "Ten Ferries". This area is a newly developed tourist spot, known for its beautiful natural landscape. Standing along the two banks of the 15km-long karst valley are numerous steep peaks, which, together with clear waters, make the place look like a gallery of splashed-ink landscape paintings. Rocks of all comprehensible shapes can be found here, varying with one another for beauty and grotesqueness, resembling a bat, a bamboo shoot, a pen-holder or a human figure. Each ferry has its special attractions. For instance, the outdoor bathing place at the sixth ferry, the Buddha-Seeing Terrace (Wangfoting) and the boating place at the ninth ferry, and the huge Chinese character "佛" (Buddha) carved on the rock of Mt. Longshan at the tenth ferry are all very fascinating. The ninth ferry is the center of this area.

Ice-Lanterns at the Longqing Gorge

Longqing Gorge

The gorge stands in the mountainous region of Yanqing County, about 80 km to the north of Beijing. A natural canyon flanked on both sides by green peaks of grotesque shapes, the gorge has become more beautiful following the construction in 1981 of the Gucheng Reservoir. Standing on the 70m-tall water dam, and looking around from this vantage point, the visitor will see the spectacular scene of a smooth lake lying among high mountains. If he comes into the gorge, the zigzag route he follows will make him feel as if he were passing through the Three Gorges in the Changjiang River, and the towering peaks and blue water there will make him feel as if he were travelling along the Lijiang River at Guilin. Chief among the tourists' attractions are Mt. Cockscomb (Mt. Jiguan). Magic Pen Peak (Shenbifeng) and Buddhist Warrior Temple (Jingangsi).Pleasantly cool in summer, with a temperature 6℃ lower than in urban Beijing, this area makes an ideal summer resort. It is also the place where the attractive ice-lantern party is held annually because the freezing period in this area is as long as six months.

The Scenes in the Longqing Gorge

White Dragon Pool

The pool is situated in an area to the southeast of the Miyun Reservoir, about 25km from the county city of Miyun. With numerous springs and streams, of which the pool is the fountainhead, the area has been known since ancient times as a land of waters. In addition, there are grotesque rocks and thick woods here, which present a beautiful scenery. In the past, people would come here to pray for rain, for this area was thought to be the dwelling place of deities. On their way to their mountain villa at Chengde, the Qing emperors would make short stays here. In recent years, while old buildings have been completely renovated, such as the Temple of Five Cereals (Wuguci) of the Yuan Dynasty and the Dragon Spring Temple (Longquansi) of the Ming Dynasty, new buildings — villas and castles — have been put up for visitors, too.

Grand View Garden

Situated on the moat in the southwestern corner of Beijing, the garden is a reconstruction of the Grand View Garden described in the world-famous novel *A Dream of the Red Mansion* — a garden "complete with scenes both on earth and in heaven, and laid out in an exquisitely designed landscape", a garden epitomizing the arts of garden building of ancient China. The reconstruction covers an area of 125,000m², consisting of scenic spots such as Yihong Courtyard, Xiaoxiang Courtyard, Qiushuang Study, Grand-view Tower, Longcui Nunnery and Daoxiang Village. The landscape, woods, flowers and indoor furnishings all have a strong artistic charm.

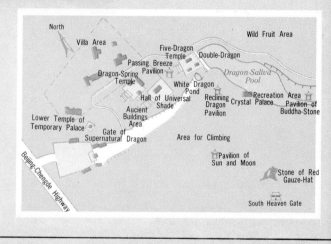

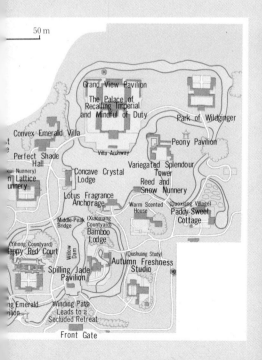

MOUNTAIN OF HEAVENLY LONGEVITY

Awl-shaped Stone Pass

Tailing Tomb

Kangling Tomb

Tailing Village

Kangling Village

Maoling Tomb

Swallow Mountain Pass

Maoling Village

Yuling Tomb

Temple of Nether World Lao-tse Hall

Qingling Tomb

Yuling Village

Qingling Village

Xianling Tomb

Changling Tomb

Jingling Tomb

Dingling Tomb

Xianling Village

Jingling Village

Victory Mountain Pass

Zhaoling Tomb

Yongling Tomb

Deling Tomb

International
Friendship Forest

The Airport of
Tourism in the Sky

Zhaoling Village

Yongling Village

Deling Village

Ten-Thousand-Madam Tomb

Beixin Village

Siling Tomb

Tailing Garden

Huzhuang Village

Beijing International
Golf Course

Mourning House at Tombs

Xiaogong Gate

Window Lattice Gate

Kangling Garden

Changling Garden

Stele Pavilion

The Way of Stone Figures

Ming Tombs Reservoir

The Monument of
the Ming Tomb Reservoir

est Mountain Pass

Tiger Mt.

Dagong Gate

Nanxin Village

Immortal Cave

Dagong Gate

Jiantou Village

Dragon Hill

Chao'an Wan Village

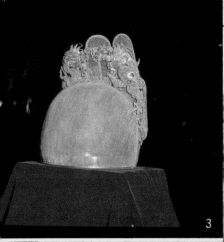

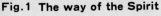

Fig.1 **The way of the Spirit**

Fig.2 **The Underground Palace**

Fig.3 **Gold Crown for Emperor**

Fig.4 **Phoenix Crown for
        Empresses**

VISITED 20/8/92

Ming Tombs

There are altogether 13 tombs for 13 emperors of the Ming Dynasty. These tombs are situated at the southern foot of Mt. Longevity of Heaven (Tianshoushan) in Changping County, 50km away from Beijing, in a basin with a south-facing opening, covering an area of 4,000,000m². For over 200 years starting from the 7th year of the Yongle reign period of the Ming Dynasty (1409), when the construction work began, the tomb area was a forbidden zone for the average people. The area is entered by a huge stone gateway, which is an excellent work of carving of ancient China. Leading from the gateway is a 750m−long path, flanked by stele pavilions and 18 pairs of lifelike stone statues. Further down the path stands the Gate to Heaven (Tianmen), which, according to legend, the dead is to pass to go to heaven. There is a seven-arch stone bridge beyond, and a little distance

from the bridge is Changling, the tomb for the Ming emperor, Yongle and his wife. It is the earliest and also the largest of the 13 Ming tombs, consisting of the Hall of Great Favour (Ling'en Hall), the Open Tower (Minglou), the Treasure City (Baocheng) and the underground palace. The Hall of Great Favour is the largest ancient wood construction in China, supported by 32 magnificent nanmu (Pheobe nanmu) pillars. Southwest of Changling is Dingling, the burial place of the 13th Ming emperor, Zhu Yijun, and his two wives. It was excavated in 1956, and this brought to light the mystery of the underground palace. Unearthed from this tomb were more than 3000 precious cultural relics, including gold crowns and dragon-decorated robes. Southeast of the tomb area is a newly developed scenic spot, the Shisanling Reservoir.

33

Lugou(Marco Polo) Bridge

Sitting over the Yongding River (Permanent Stability River), which is 15km to the southwest of Beijing, is the Lugou Bridge, or known to foreigners as the Marco Polo Bridge. It is a multi-arch stone bridge which is the oldest and most magnificent of similar constructions in the area of Beijing. The bridge started to be built in the 29th year of the Dading reign period of the Jin Dynasty (1189), in an area which has been a strategic passage between Jicheng, the capital of the State of Yan, and the North China Plain way back to the Warring States period (475—221 BC). East of the bridge stands a pavilion housing an imperial stele with an inscription by Emperor Qianlong of the Qing Dynasty—"the Moon at Dawn over Lugou". The bridge has 11 arches and is more than 260m in length. Carved on the 140 balusters are 485 stone lions of different sizes and in different postures. The ancient City of Wanping nearby was constructed in the 13th year of the Chongzhen reign period (1640). It is here, on July 7th, 1937, that the Chinese army fired the first shot against Japanese invaders, thus raising the curtain on the great war of resistance against Japan. An exhibition hall has been built here in memory of the war.

The Moon at Dawn over Lug

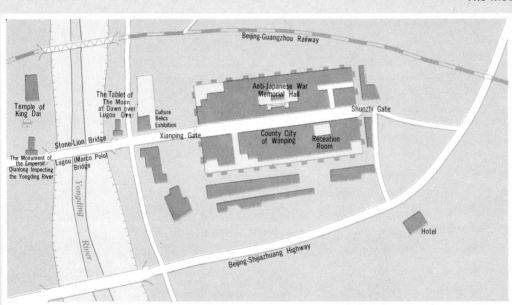

Lugou (Marco Polo) Bridge

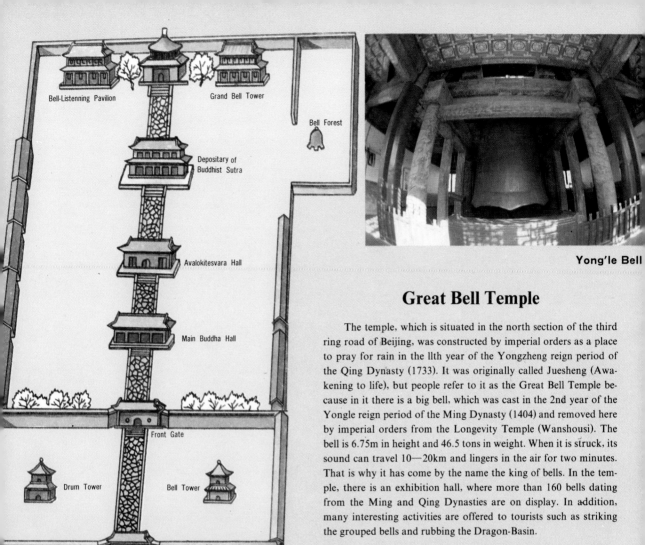

Bell-Listenning Pavilion

Grand Bell Tower

Bell Forest

Depositary of Buddhist Sutra

Avalokitesvara Hall

Main Buddha Hall

Front Gate

Drum Tower

Bell Tower

Gate

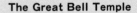

Yong'le Bell

Great Bell Temple

The temple, which is situated in the north section of the third ring road of Beijing, was constructed by imperial orders as a place to pray for rain in the llth year of the Yongzheng reign period of the Qing Dynasty (1733). It was originally called Juesheng (Awakening to life), but people refer to it as the Great Bell Temple because in it there is a big bell, which was cast in the 2nd year of the Yongle reign period of the Ming Dynasty (1404) and removed here by imperial orders from the Longevity Temple (Wanshousi). The bell is 6.75m in height and 46.5 tons in weight. When it is struck, its sound can travel 10—20km and lingers in the air for two minutes. That is why it has come by the name the king of bells. In the temple, there is an exhibition hall, where more than 160 bells dating from the Ming and Qing Dynasties are on display. In addition, many interesting activities are offered to tourists such as striking the grouped bells and rubbing the Dragon-Basin.

The Great Bell Temple

15   Beacon Tower
14

13

12

11

10

9

8

7

6   5   4   3   2   1

Lotus Pond

Cable Car

The Way for Climbing the City Wall

Pearl Spring

Dragon Pool

Foreign Friends Restaurant

Restaurant

Yanjing Studio

No.1 Parking Lot

Ticket Office

Ticket Office

Mandarin-Duck Pine

Guest-Welcoming Pine

No.2 Parking Lot

Mutianyu Village

Tourist Office of Mutianyu

VISITED 22/8/92

The Great Wall at Mutianyu

The Mutianyu section of the Great wall, also a vital part of the defence system of the capital during the Ming Dynasty, is located in the mountainous region of Huairou County, 70km northeast of Beijing, connecting with the Juyong Pass in the west and Gubeikou in the east. Renovated in recent years, it is now open to the public, and is known as the second Badaling for its scenery. This section was built in the early Ming Dynasty on the foundation of the wall put up by the State of Northern Qi (550—577). It has a large number of guard towers, as evidenced by the fact that 22 beacon towers spread along a length of 2km. This is a feature that attracts visitors. In addition, there are such spectacles as the convergence of three walls and juxtaposition of three beacon towers. Among the verdant woods there are ancient pines and mountain springs. A footpath has been built for climbers and a cable-car service is available.

36

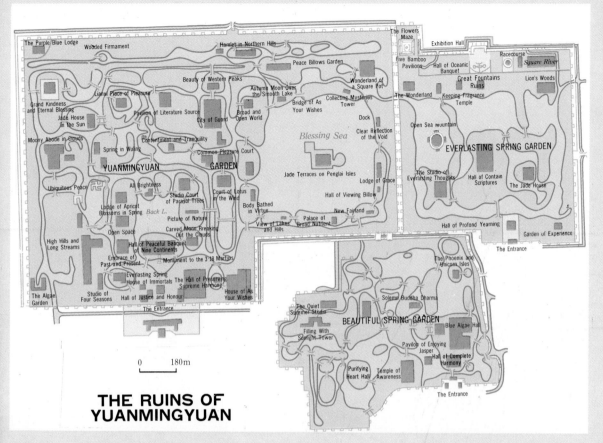

The map labels (reading across the image):

The Purple Blue Lodge · Wooded Firmament · Hamlet in Northern Hills · The Flowers Maze · Exhibition Hall · Five Bamboo Pavilions · Hall of Oceanic Banquet · Racecourse · Square River · Peace Billows Garden · Beauty of Western Peaks · Wonderland of a Square Pot · Great Fountains Ruins · Lion's Woods · Autumn Moon Over the Smooth Lake · Collecting Mysteries Tower · Lianxi Place of Pleasure · The Wonderland · Keeping Fragrance Temple · Grand Kindness and Eternal Blessing · Pavilion of Literature Source · Broad and Open World · Bridge of As Your Wishes · Dock · Jade House in the Sun · City of Guard · Clear Reflection of the Void · Open Sea mountain · Moony Abode in Clouds · Confinement and Tranquility · Blessing Sea · Spring in Wuling · Common Pleasure Court · EVERLASTING SPRING GARDEN · YUANMINGYUAN GARDEN · Jade Terraces on Penglai Isles · The Studio of Everlasting Thoughts · Hall of Contain Scriptures · The Jade House · Ubiquitous Peace · All Brightness · Court of Lotus in the Wind · Lodge of Grace · Studio Court of Parasol Trees · Hall of Viewing Billow · Lodge of Apricot Blossoms in Spring · Back L. · Picture of Nature · Body Bathed in Virtue · New Fairland · Open Space · Carved Moon Breaking Out the Clouds · View of Lakes and Hills · Palace of Broad Nutrient · Hall of Profond Yearning · High Hills and Long Streams · Hall of Peaceful Banquet of Nine Continents · Garden of Experience · Embrace of Past and Present · Monument to the 3.18 Martyrs · The Entrance · Everlasting Spring House of Immortals · The Hall of Preserving Supreme Harmony · House of As Your Wishes · The Algae Garden · Studio of Four Seasons · Hall of Justice and Honour · The Entrance · The Phoenix and Unicorn Isles · Solemn Buddha Dharma · The Quiet Summer Studio · BEAUTIFUL SPRING GARDEN · Blue Algae Hall · Filling With Sunlight Tower · Pavilion of Enjoying Jasper · Hall of Complete Harmony · Purifying Heart Hall · Temple of Awareness · The Entrance

0   180m

THE RUINS OF YUANMINGYUAN

Ruins of Yuanmingyuan

Located in the east of Haidian District of Beijing, it was the world-famous royal garden, which took 150 years to construct when the Qing Dynasty was at the peak of prosperity, with man power and materials supplied across the whole country. The garden consisted of the Everlasting Spring Garden (Changchunyuan) and the Beautiful Spring Garden (Yichunyuan). It covered an area of 3.47 million m², mirroring the best of traditional garden-building arts of China, and boasting a large collection of grotesque rocks and exotic flowers. There are more than a hundred scenic spots, which were constructed either in imitation of well-known gardens in South China or in an European style, hence its name "the garden of all gardens". In addition, there was a large store of precious works of art, books and cultural objects, which turned it literally into a treasure trove of culture. Unfortunately, it was looted and burned down first by the Anglo-French joint forces in 1860, and then by the allied forces of the Eight Powers in 1900. After 1949, the ruins were taken under state protection. As a result of large-scale afforestation and the effort to sort out the ruins, the place has been developed into a park where visitors can see the ruins and a few renovated places such as the Gate of the Ten Thousand Springs Garden. In the Everlasting Spring Garden, an exhibition is held.

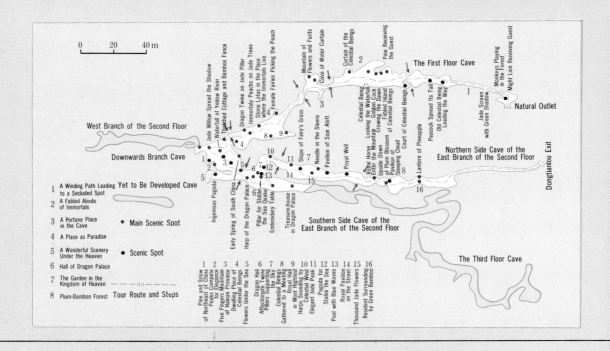

Zhoukoudian—Home of the "Peking Man"

Zhoukoudian is some 50km to the southwest of Beijing. It was here, in the limestone cavern on Mt. Longgu, that the Peking Man lived and kept his kindling material 578,000 years ago. Following the discovery in 1929 of a Peking Man's skull by the Chinese Palaeontologist, Pei Wenzhong, fossils of about 40 Peking Men and over 100 animals they had eaten were sorted out by other scientists from the heaps in the cavern, and the discoveries of a large number of stone wares and signs suggest the use of fire. All this confirms the fact that the "Peking Man" lived in the cavern for as long as 300,000 years. Relics of the "Upper Cave Man", the primitive yellow man of 18,000 years ago, have also been found in a cave above the "Peking Man" cavern. Now the place is a research center of paleontology and paleoanthropology. There is an exhibition hall there, which is open to the public.

Peking Man Cave

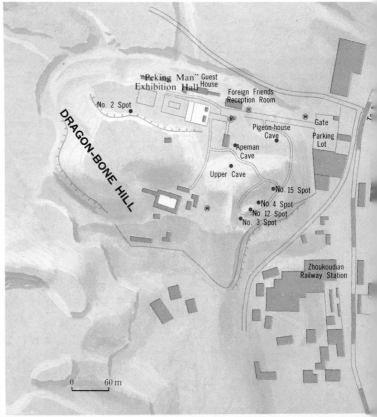

Stone—Flower Cave

Located in Fangshan 56km west of Beijing, it is a deep
[ka]rst cave, which is rarely seen in north China. It was first
[dis]covered by a roaming Baddhist master of the Ming Dyn-
[ast]y, Qiuyuan Guangfa, who gave it the name Qianzhen
[Ca]ve and put up a Buddhist statue in it. This is why the cave
[is a]lso referred to as the Stone Buddha Cave. So far two lev-
[els] of the cave are open to the public. This part of the cave
[has] a total length of 1,360m, consisting of 11 halls, 14 cham-
[be]rs, 63 branch caves and 14 scenic spots. In the
[Bu]ddha-Worshipping Hall at the entrance of the cave are
[se]t a large number of stone carvings. Inside the cave, there
[are] colourful stalagmites and stalactites of different shapes,
[wh]ich look like various things such as lotus flower and wat-
[erfa]ll, and form a long corridor at one point, and a labyrinth
[at] another. All this gives the place an atmosphere of the
[wo]nderland.

Stone Flower Cave

Stupa for Tooth Relic of Buddha

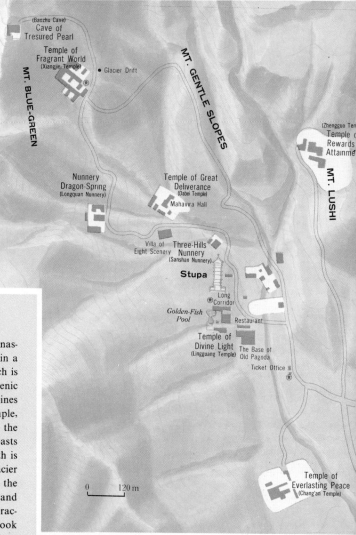

Eight Scenic Spots at Western Hills

The eight scenic spots refer to eight ancient temples built in dynas-
[ties] following the Tang and Song. These temples are all situated in a
[par]k in Shijingshan District to the west of Beijing — a park which is
[wel]l known for the lush growth of woods and flowers. The first scenic
[spo]t is Chang'an Temple, which attracts visitors with lacebark pines
[goi]ng back to the Yuan Dynasty; the second is Lingguang Temple,
[whi]ch is noted for the pagoda housing the tooth relic of Buddha; the
[thir]d is Sanshan Nunnery; the fourth is Dabei Temple, which boasts
[work]s from the Jin and Yuan Dynasties, Buddhist statues; the fifth is
[Lon]gquan Temple whose attractions are cool spring water and glacier
[reli]c; the sixth is Xiangjie Temple where there are magnolia from the
[Min]g and the palace for short stays for Emperors Kangxi and
[Qia]nlong; the seventh is Baozhu Cave where the monk, Haixiu, prac-
[tise]d Buddhism; there is a pavilion on the mountain for people to look
[i]nto the distance from a vartage point; the eighth is Zhengguo Tem-
[ple] which is famous for a Buddhist meditation room with a winding
[path] leading to it and a stone chamber cut in a cliff.

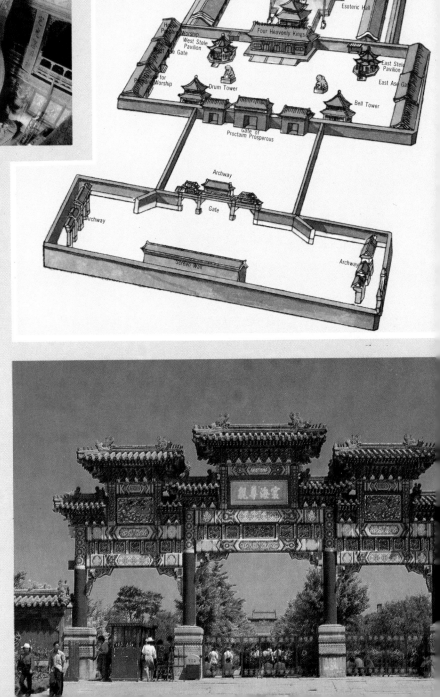

Lama Temple
(Yonghegong Lamasery)

Located in the northeast corner of the urban area of Beijing, it is the largest lamasery in the city. It was constructed in the 33rd year of the Kangxi reign period of the Qing Dynasty (1694) as an official residence for Yongzheng before he came to the throne, and was the birthplace of Emperor Qianlong. In the 9th year of the Qianlong reign period of the Qing Dynasty (1744), it was turned into a lamasery. It comprises five major halls , all imposing and magnificent, bespeaking an integration of different architectural styles of the Han, Man, Monglian and Tibetan nationalities. There is a rich store of religious articles in the lamasery; chief among them are the statue of Maitreya, carved out of a 26m long single piece of sandal wood, the Buddha niche made of nanmu and the 500 arhats made of five metals—gold, silver, bronze, iron and tin. The three of them are referred to as the three treasures. There are also many murals based on religious themes in the halls.

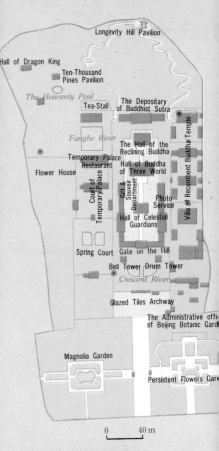

Longevity Hill Pavilion
Hall of Dragon King
Ten-Thousand Pines Pavilion
The Heavenly Pool
Tea-Stall
The Depositary of Buddhist Sutra
Fanghe River
Temporary Palace Restaurant
The Hall of the Reclining Buddha
Hall of Buddha of Three World
Flower House
Court of Temporary Palace
Gift & Souvenir Department
Photo Service
Villa of Recumbent Buddha Temple
Hall of Celestial Guardians
Spring Court
Gate on the Hill
Bell Tower Drum Tower
Crescent River
Glazed Tiles Archway
The Administrative offi of Beijing Botanic Gard
Magnolia Garden
Persistent Flowers Gar

0   40 m

Temple of Reclining Buddha

Constructed in the Zhenguan reign period of the Tang Dynasty (629—649), the temple lies at the southern foot of Mt. Shou'an to the north of Fragrant Hills, facing south and composed of three courtyards. In the middle courtyard, buildings are harmoniously laid out, such as the glazed archway and the sutra-storing hall. The giant sleeping Buddha is housed in the hall in the courtyard at the rear. The statue was cast in the lst year of the Zhizhi reign period of the Yuan Dynasty (1321), and altogether 250,000kg of bronze was used for this purpose. 5.2m in length, the Buddha lies on his side in a natural posture and with a calm facial expression, surrounded by his twelve disciples. This is the scene of Sakyamuni consoling all living creatures before his entry into nirvana. To the northwest of the temple are a montane garden and a summer resort — the Cherry Dale. Southeast of temple is the memorial hall of Cao Xueqin, author of the famous novel *A Dream of the Red Mansion*.

Deer Park

Camel

Mou
Ze

Giraffe
House

Asiatic
Wild Ass

Tropical Fishes
House

Mountain
Gazelle

Gibbon

Wild Yak

Orangutan

Golden Fish

Sea
Animals
Pool

Takin

Sea
Animals
House

Amphibian and
Reptile House

Recreation Room

Auto-plane

Children Zoo

Toy of
Seachair

BEIJING ZOO

The zoo is located outside Xizhimen of Beijing. During the Ming Dynasty, it was a royal manor. In the late Qing times, it was an experimental field for farming arts, and a zoo was put up here. After 1949, it was officially given the name "Beijing Zoo". A lot of constructions have been built ever since for monkeys, elephants, bears, tigers and lions, deer, hippos, reptiles, pandas, aquatic fowls and small animals. The collection of animals here has been growing both in species and in quantity. One can see here animals peculiar to China such as giant pandas, golden-hair monkeys, tufted deer, wild horses, white-lipped deer, pheasants and red-crowned cranes, and also exotic animals from other parts of the world such as mask oxen, gorillas, polar bears, giraffes, African elephants, ostriches and penguins.

Temple of Pool and Cudrania

The temple, located in the mountainous region of Mentougou 45km west of Beijing, is the oldest temple in the area of Beijing. As it was constructed during the Jin Dynasty (265—316), it has a longer history than the capital. The temple is so named because of the dragon pool and the three-bristle cudrania nearby. Lying against the mountain, it faces south. Its buildings, laid out scatteredly yet harmoniously, can be divided into three groups. Those in the middle constitute the main body of the temple, with the main gate, the Mahavira Hall (Daxiong Baodian) and the Vairochana Pavilion (Piluge) all lined up on the central axis on progressively higher levels. The eastern group includes the abbot's courtyard and the temporary dwelling place of the Qing emperors. The western group is composed of the Ordination Altar (Jietan) and the Avalokitesvara Hall (Guanyindian). In front of the temple, there are a group of pagodas dating from the Jin, Ming and Qing Dynasties. Inside the temple, there are rare plants such as magnolia and king tree.

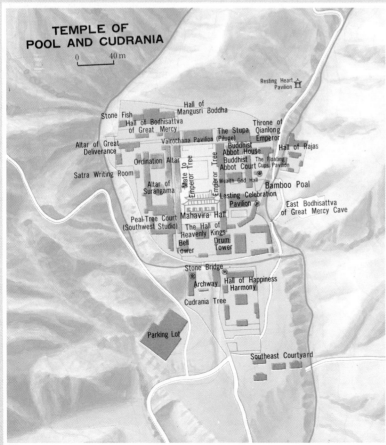

TEMPLE OF POOL AND CUDRANIA

0   40 m

- Resting Heart Pavilion
- Stone Fish
- Hall of Mangusri Boddha
- Hall of Bodhisattva of Great Mercy
- Throne of Qianlong Emperor
- The Stupa (Piluge)
- Vairochana Pavilion
- Altar of Great Deliverance
- Buddhist Abbot House
- Hall of Rajas
- Ordination Altar
- Buddhist Abbot Court
- The Floating Cups Pavilion
- Satra Writing Room
- Gate to Emperor Tree
- Emperor Tree
- Wealth God Hall
- Altar of Surangama
- Lasting Celebration Pavilion
- Bamboo Poal
- East Bodhisattva of Great Mercy Cave
- Peal-Tree Court (Southwest Studio)
- Mahavira Hall
- The Hall of Heavenly Kings
- Bell Tower
- Drum Tower
- Stone Bridge
- Archway
- Hall of Happiness Harmony
- Cudrania Tree
- Parking Lot
- Southeast Courtyard

Temple of Ordination Terrace

TEMPLE OF ORDINATION TERRACE

0   40 m

Parking Lot

Wealth God Hall

Ginkgo
Embracing Pagoda Pine
Hall of Rajas   Pagoda of
Liao Dynasty
Nine-Dragon Pine
Hall of Great
Deliverance

Ordination Altar Hall

House of
Gathering-Wisdom   Ginkgo

Administrative office

Hall of
Master Guan   Hall of Bell Tower
Sangharama

Peony Courtyard

Golden Stele   Hall of
Sleeping Dragon Pine   The Hall of   Temple Gate
Heavenly Kings   Gate of the
Pavilion of   Temple
One-Thousaud   Mahavira Hall   Drum Tower   Gate
Hall of Boddisattva Buddhas   The Founders Hall
of Great Mercy   Carefree Pine
Hall of Nine   Hall of   South-Palace
Prayers   Purifying Heart   Court

Hall Master Guan   Moving Pine

East Court
of Motionless
Buddhist Abbot Court

Lower Court

Upper Court

Temple of Ordination Terrace

Lay in the middle of Horse Saddle Hill (Ma'anshan), it is about 35km from the capital. It was constructed in 622 in the Tang Dynasty, and renovated and expanded on many occasions during the Ming Dynasty. The main hall of the temple is the Hall of Mahavira (Daxiong Baodian), behind which stands the Pavilion of One Thousand Buddhas (Qianfoge). According to legend, the eminent monk of the Liao Dynasty, Fa Jun, presided over the ordination ceremony on the terrace here, which is 3.5m in height, made of white marble, exquisitely carved, with a niche housing various coloured Buddhist statues. This terrace and two others — one in Zhaoqing Temple of Hangzhou and one in Kaiyuan Temple of Quanzhou — are listed as the three major ordination terraces in China. Northeast of the temple is the pagoda yard where many ancient pagodas from the Liao and Yuan Dynasties are kept. In front of the Hall of Brilliant Kings (Mingwangdian) there is a stone pillar, which is exquisitely carved with Buddhist images and sutras. The temple is famous for its ancient pines, which bear interesting names such as Moving Pine, Sleeping Dragon Pine, Carefree Pine, Nine-Dragon Pine and Embracing Pagoda Pine. The oldest is the Nine-Dragon Pine, which has a history of over 1300 years.

Main Shopping Areas

Beijing is a major shopping centre of China with densely concentrated business network, rich in products of diversified variety.

The major shopping areas are located in Qianmen, Wangfujing, Xidan, Dongdan, Dongsi, etc. Famous shopping centres in these areas include Beijing Department Store, Dong'an Bazaar, Xidan Department Store, Longfu Shopping Mension, and Many Friendship Stores for the convenience of foreign visitors as well as the overseas, Taiwan and Hong Kong visitors. In addition, there are over forty local business centres spreading in the suburb and its vicinities around Beijing to satisfy the various needs of all visitors. For those who are interested in ancient books, antiques, traditional stationeries (the four treasures of the study) and famous paintings and calligraphies, the cultural street of Liulichang out of the Hepingmen is an ideal place to go.

Beijing is also the display window of all the best special products from all over China, all the local provinces and cities send the best of their products here for display and sales. The art and craft works of Beijing are famous all over the world. Among them are the cloisonne enamel articles, jade carvings, ivory carvings, lacquer works, palace lanterns, silk flowers, carpets — the favorites of all overseas visitors.

The over-all selling total of Beijing tops over all the other cities of China, for besides serving the needs of over 10 million local citizens, it has also to satisfy the needs of over a million of floating population and tens of thousands of foreign visitors.

We warmly welcome our foreign friends to come shopping in Beijing and we will assure you of our most satisfying service.

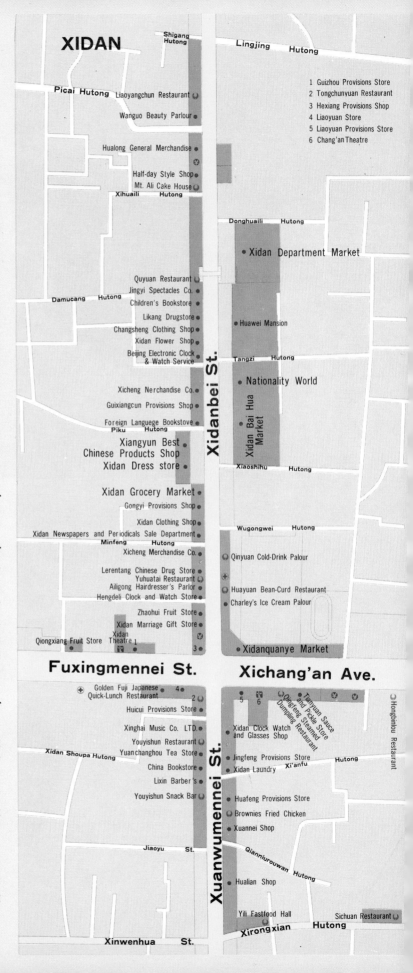

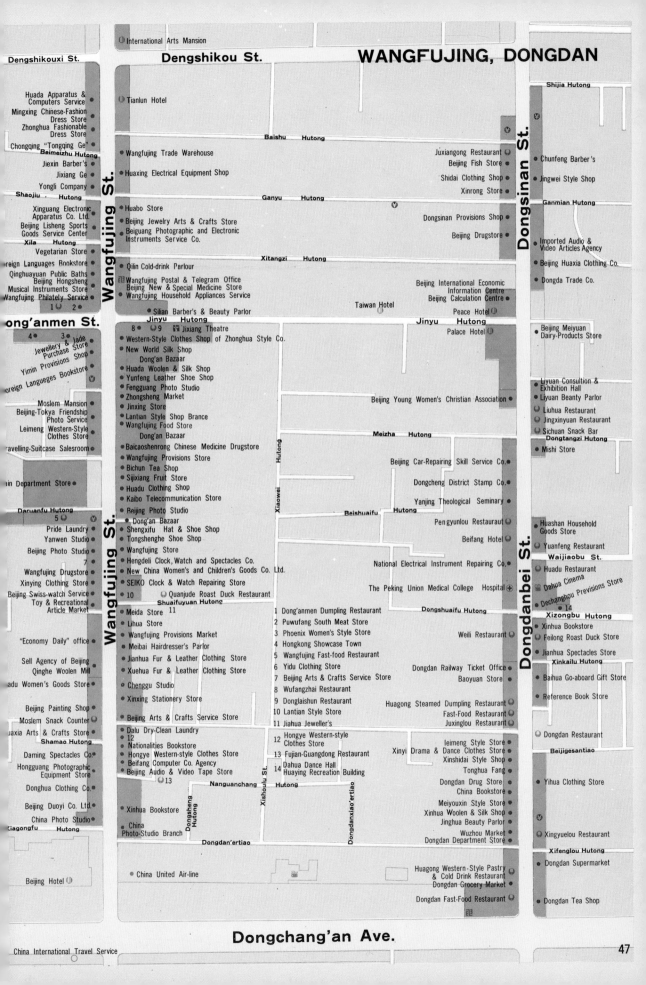

QIANMEN, DASHANLAN

Qianmenxi St.

Zhengyang Gate

Qianmendong St.

Taifenglou Restaurant
Dongfang Pearl Restaurant
Lixin Shop
Huadu Artist Gallery
Riyuetan Department Store
Tea House
Tianlian Bazaar
The Great Wall Restaurant
Zhengyang Provisions Store
Kentucky Fried Chicken Restaurant
Tiangong Restaurant
Qianmen Provisions Shop
Bazaar of Tea House Commerce and Trade Bloc

Qianmen Arrow Tower

Beijing Railway Worker's Club
Qianmen Railway Ticket Office

Lidu Restaurant
Hongguang Beauty Parlour
Zhengyanglou Restaurant
Huakang Provisions Shop
Huayi Store

Qianmen xiheyan St.

Xingbao Gold Shop
Xuanwu Qiaoya Bazaar
Hongmao Store

Xidamochang St.

Xinxin Style Shop
Beijing Acoustic Technology Service
Qianmen Tourist Shop
Zhongyuan Photo Studio

Yueshengzhai Provisions Shop
Beijing Silk Shop

Daqianmen Shop
Dabei Photo Studio
Tourist-bus Ticket Office
Qianmen Fruit Shop
Qianmen Musical Instruments Shop
Qinglinchun Tea Store
Fengxian Meat Shop
Tongsanyi Provisions Store
Guanghe Theatre
Changchuntang Chinese Drugstore

Modern Bazaar
Guangda Trading Co.
Huafu Clock & Watch Shop
Qianmen Dairy Products Shop
Jingrong Clothing Store

Langfang'ertiao

Lili Restaurant
Quanjude Roast Duck Restaurant
Qianmen Drugstore
Duyichu Steamed Dumpling Restaurant
Tiancheng Shoeshop
Bianyifang Roast Duck Restaurant

Tonghexuan Restaurant
Beijing Folk Art Hall
No.2 Dashanlan Bazaar
Huale Shop
Jingcheng Fashionable Dress Co.
Dashanlan Provisions Market
Tianma Photgraphy Service Centre

No.1 Dashanlan Bazaar
Xinhua Department Market
Dongsheng Shoe Shop
Rifuxiang Silk Shop
Qingda Fashionable Dress Store
Qianmen Women's Clothes Shop

Xianyukou St.

Yunnan Shop

Dashanlan St.

Meishi St.

Beijing Huifeng Trading Co.

Cuihua Barber's Shop
Capital Photo Studio
Maiyuan Hat Store
Daoxiangcun Provisions Shop

Fangxiang Tea Store
Dashanlan Bicycle Shop
Daguanlou Cinema
Neiliansheng Shoe Shop
Xinshidai Women' & Children's Articles Co.
Capital Color Photography Hall

Tongrentang Chinese Drugstore
Zhangyiyuan Tea Store
Xinshidai Children's Articles Shop
Hengdeli Clock & Watch Store
Chenguang Spectacles Shop

Zhimeizhai Restaurant

Qianmendajie Provisions Market
Laozhenxing Restaurant
Children's Bookstore
Pride Laundry
Beibingyang Provisions Shop
Qianmen Merchandise Shop

Dashanlanxi St.
Xiaoli Hutong
Hongmei Clothing Store
Jingda Department Market
Fangxiang Provisions Shop

Meishi St.

Dajiang Hutong

Qianmen St.

Liubu Sauce and Pickle Store

Wangpi Hutong
Feitian Middle & Old Aged Clothing Store

Yizhao Shop
Jinlong Market
Guangming Provisions Shop
Qianmen Barber House

Caijia Hutong
Zhengyang Style Co.

Shijia Hutong
Qianmen Electronic Apparatus Store
Sale Department of Beijing Radio Factory

Selling Agency of Beijing Sanhuan Woolen Co.
Qianmen Bookstore
Qianmendajie Grocery
Qianmen Quick-Lunch Restaurant

Zhangshan Hutong
Qianmen Household Appliances Shop

Post Office
Qianmen Paints and Chemical Products Shop
Sell Agency of Beijing Spectacles Co.
Jewellery & Jade Purchasing Station

Yunju Hutong
Jingxiang Articles of Daily Use Co.
Zilan Style Store

Shijing Hutong

Dajiang Laundry
Xindabei Photo Studio
Sale Department of Beijing Chinese Musical Instrument Factory

Qianmen Bicycle Shop

Ganjing Hutong
Beijing Furniture Store
Yikang Provisions Shop

Qianmen Hardware Store
Service Centre of Beijing Clock & Watch Co.

Qianmen Trade and Trust Co.
Dahua Clothing Store

Zhumao Hutong
Zhujia Hutong

1 Huabeilou Restaurant
2 Qianmen Stationery Shop
3 Zhubaoshi Bazaar
4 Shengxifu Hat & Shoe Shop
5 Jingcheng General Merchandise
6 Science & Technoloy Bookstore
7 Xinhua Bookstore
8 Beijing Arts & Crafts Shop
9 Yiqun Local Well-known & High-class Products Store
10 Buyingzhai Shoe Store
11 Wanlong Department Market
12 Yong'an Tea Store

Wholesale Department of Tong Ren Tang Chinese Drug Store

Zhushikouxi St.

Zhizhulin Restaurant
Zhushikou Cinema
Zhushikou Market

Sixin Hat & Shoe Store

Zhushikoudong St.

Chongwen District Stomatology Clinic
Sentai Tea Store
Minyue Quick-Lunch Restaurant
Fukang Drugstore

48

The Antique Shop Area
——Liulichang (Glaze Factory)

Situated outside Hepingmen, the Antique Shop Area — Liulichang is 750m long. With a long history, it is usually called "the street of displaying the cream of Chinese culture". Many factories manufacturing glazed products were set up here from the Yuan Dynasty. During the Ming Dynasty, most of glazed articles were from this area for building up palaces, so getting the name of Liulichang (Glaze Factory). Since the Qing Dynasty, the area gradually

turned into a market of ancient books, arts and antiques, and the Antique Shop Area began to rise. The area resumed its traditional look by restoration in recent years. Now, there are dozens of shops here running the ancient books, gold, jade and pottery wares, calligraphys and paintings, the four treasures of the study and so on. All the facades of shops are very exquisite, such as painted and carved ridgepoles and beams, inscribed boards horizontally hanged above the doors, ingeniously decorated windows. The rooms insides shops are multicolorfully and antiquely furnished. The area is really a good place to these who love the Chinese culture.

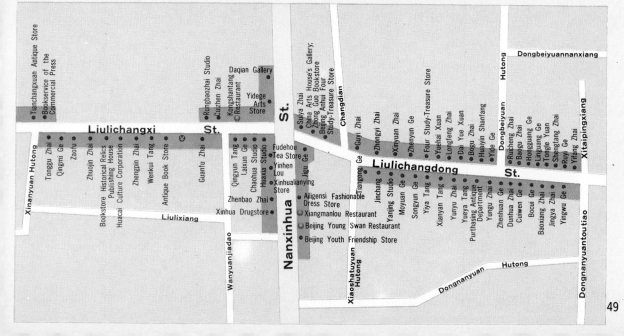

International Airport

Sanyuan Flyover

NEW APPEARENCE

Jianguomen Ave.

OF BEIJING

Tuanjiehu Resident Area

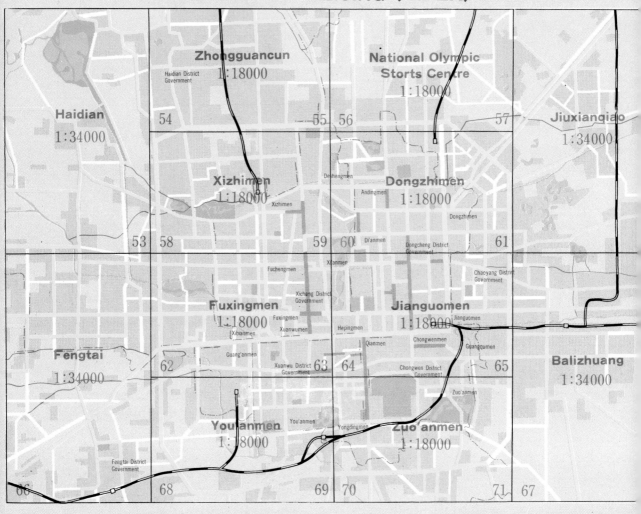

A City Changing Every Day

Althouth Beijing has been the capital of China for almost 800 years, it was just a consumer–city serving feudal emperors and bureaucrat compradors before 1949. Its construction level was as low as that of old capitals of Middle Ages.

Since 1949, Beijing has made great advances in urban construction. The color–lost historical and cultural old city has revived to its youth. Now Beijing, as a modern city with ancient capital style and features, has all kinds of city functions, many huge modern buildings and advanced foundational facilities. It stands erect in major capitals of the world.

Urban construction of Beijing is developing rapidly. There are hundreds of great public buildings in Beijing, among which built in recent ten years are new Beijing Libarary, Diaoyutai State Guesthouse, China Theatre, China International Exhibition Center and many hotels such as Great Wall Hotel, Kunlun Hotel, Holiday Inn Lido Beijing, Xiyuan Hotel and International Hotel. Together with the Great Hall of the People, the Museum of Chines Revolution and History, the Cultural Palace of the Na tionalities, National Agricultural Exhibition Centre, China Art Gallery and Beijing Railway Station, they make the ol city full of spirit. Various buildings built in the past fort years cover an area of 150,000,000 m², seven times that o the old city. More than 120 residential quarters were con structed which cover an area of over 30,000 m². The cit expanded its urban area from original 109 km² to 75 km², constructed highway of 2900 km, 500 km longer tha the distance from Beijing to Guangzhou. Ring roads an radiating roads together with more that 23 modern flyover make it possible to go in all directions into or out of th city. Elementarily municipal facilities for supplying wate power, gas, heat, communication and postal services ha been set up in order to enhance city functions as a capita Beijing has been much improved in environmental sanita tion. More and more trees and flowers have been plante in and around the city Beijing, a modern metropolis, showing a picture of prosperous socialism modernizatio to the world.

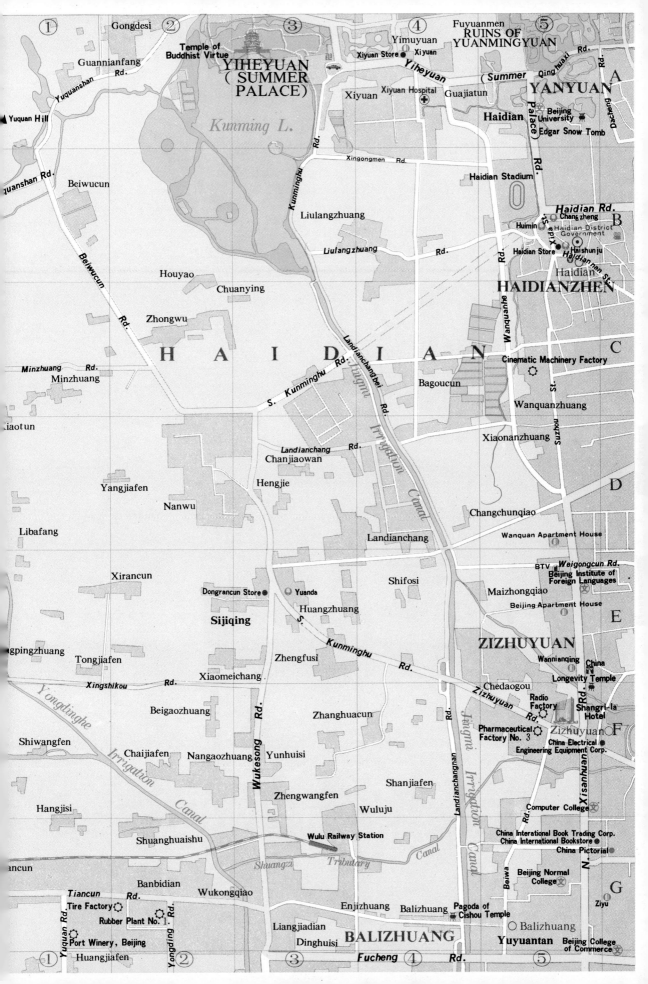

① Gongdesi ② ③ ④ Fuyuanmen ⑤

Guannianfang

Yuquanshan Rd.

Temple of Buddhist Virtue

YIHEYUAN (SUMMER PALACE)

RUINS OF YUANMINGYUAN

Yimuyuan

Xiyuan Store ● Xiyuan

Yiheyuan

(Summer

Qinghuaxi Rd.

YANYUAN

A

▲ Yuquan Hill

Kunming L.

Xiyuan

Xiyuan Hospital

Guajiatun

Haidian

Palace

Beijing University ●

Dazang

Edgar Snow Tomb

Beiwucun

Xingongmen Rd.

Haidian Stadium

Beiwucun Rd.

Houyao

Liulangzhuang

Kunminghu Rd.

Haidian Rd.

Chang zheng

St.

Huimin

Haidian District Government

B

Zhongwu

Chuanying

Liulangzhuang

Rd.

Wanquanhe

Haidian Store ● ● Haishunju

Haidian nan St.

Haidian

Minzhuang Rd.

H A I D I A N

Landianchangbei Rd.

S. Kunminghu Rd.

HAIDIANZHEN

Minzhuang

Landianchang Rd.

Bagoucun

Cinematic Machinery Factory ✿

C

Xiaotun

Yangjiafen

Landianchang

Chanjiaowan

Hengjie

Suzhou St.

Wanquanzhuang

Xiaonanzhuang

Nanwu

Irrigation Canal

Changchunqiao

D

Libafang

Landianchang

Wanquan Apartment House

Xirancun

Dongrancun Store ●

○ Yuanda

Shifosi

BTV Weigongcun Rd.
Beijing Institute of Foreign Languages

Sijiqing

Huangzhuang

S.

Maizhongqiao

Beijing Apartment House

E

gpingzhuang

Tongjiafen

Zhengfusi

Kunminghu Rd.

ZIZHUYUAN

Wannianqing

China

Longevity Temple

Xingshikou Rd.

Xiaomeichang

Chedaogou

Radio Factory

Shangri-la Hotel

Beigaozhuang

Zhanghuacun

Zizhuyuan Rd.

Pharmaceutical Factory No. 3 ✿

Zizhuyuan

F

Yongdinghe

Wukesong Rd.

Yunhuisi

Jiangna

Irrigation Canal

China Electrical ●
Engineering Equipment Corp.

Shiwangfen

Chaijiafen

Nangaozhuang

Landianchangnan Rd.

Xisanhuan Rd.

Computer College ✿

Hangjisi

Zhengwangfen

Shanjiafen

Wuluju

Beiwa

China International Book Trading Corp.
China International Bookstore ●
China Pictorial ●

Shuanghuaishu

Wulu Railway Station

Canal

Beijing Normal College ✿

rancun

Shuangzi Tributary

G

Ziyu

Banbidian

Tiancun Rd.
Tire Factory ✿

Wukongqiao

Enjizhuang Balizhuang

Pagoda of Cishou Temple

○ Balizhuang

Rubber Plant No. 1. ✿

① Yuquan Rd.

Port Winery, Beijing ✿

Huangjiafen

Yongding Rd.

② Liangjiadian

Dinghuisi

③ BALIZHUANG

Fucheng ④ Rd.

YUYUANTAN

Beijing College of Commerce ✿

⑤

① ② ③

RUINS OF YUANMINGYUAN

Qinghuaxi　Rd.

QINGHUAYUAN

Beijing
College of Forestry

Dongwangzhuang

Dachengtang
Chengfu　St.　Qinghuanan　Rd.
Zaoshuyuan
Gouyan
Chengfu

Qinghua University

Shuangqing　Rd.

Dongsheng

Edgar Snow Tomb

Lanqiying

Workers' Club, Wudaokou

YANYUAN

Chengfu　Rd.

Sancaitang

Dongsheng

Wudaokou Store

Zhongguanyuan

Dongshengyuan

Zan'anchu

Zhongguancun Agricultural
Products Market

ZHONGGUANCUN

B　**Haidian Rd.**

Zhongguancun　Rd.

Changzheng Restaurant

Xinzhuangdahutong

Haidian Serving Building
Yibinlou
Restaurant

Zhongguancun

Workers' Club,
Haidian

Haidian
District Government

Haidian Store
Haishunju

Haidianzhen

Kexuecheng Supermarket

S.　Zhongguancun　Rd.

Xiwudaokou

H　A　I　D

Yangjiajing

Haidiannan　St.

Haidian Vegetable Market
Haidian Vegetable Supermarket

HAIDIANZHEN

Taipingzhuang

Haidian
Rd.

Haidian Hospital

Haidian

C

Baita'an

CAAC Ticket Office

Camera Factory

Shuangyushu

Dazhongsi

People's University
of China

SHUANGYUSHU

Train Booking Office

Yianshan

Foodstuffs Corp. No. 1

Ancient Bell Museum
Great Bell Temple

Qingyun Instruments Factory

W.　**Beisanhuan**　Rd.

Beijing Watch Factory

Youyi

Baishiqiao
Rd.

D

Agriculture Film Studio

Friendship Guesthouse

① ② ③

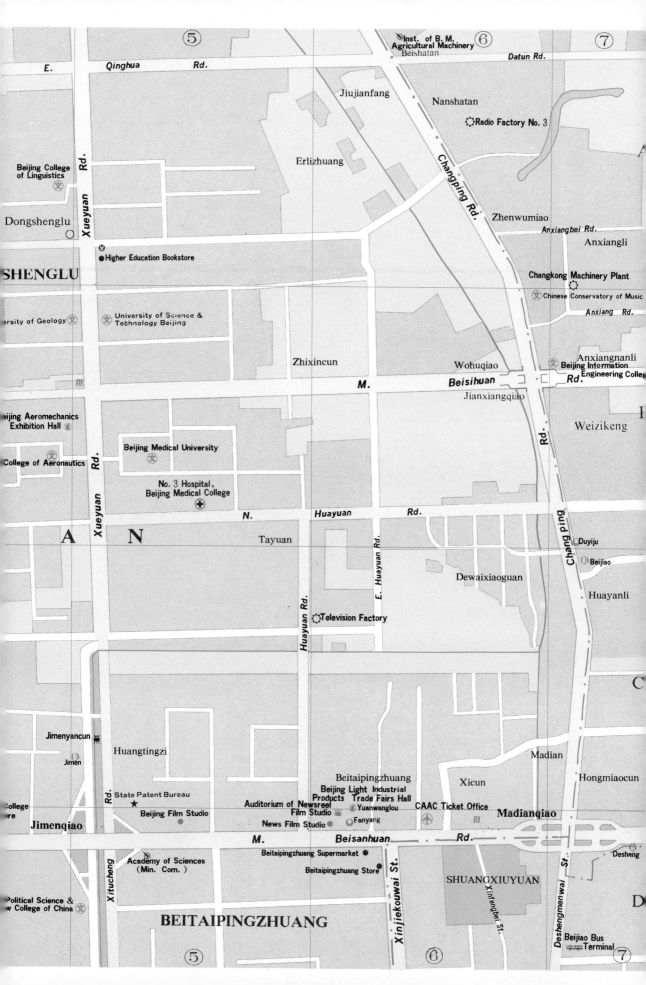

E. Qinghua Rd.

Inst. of B. M.
Agricultural Machinery
Beishatan

Datun Rd.

Jiujianfang

Nanshatan

☼ Radio Factory No. 3

Erlizhuang

Beijing College
of Linguistics ⊛

Xueyuan Rd.

Zhenwumiao

Dongshenglu ○

Anxiangbei Rd.

Anxiangli

⊛ Higher Education Bookstore

SHENGLU

Changkong Machinery Plant

⊛ Chinese Conservatory of Music

University of Geology ⊛

⊛ University of Science &
Technology Beijing

Anxiang Rd.

Zhixincun

Wohuqiao

Anxiangnanli
⊛ Beijing Information
Engineering Colleg

M.

Beisihuan

Rd.

Jianxiangqiao

Beijing Aeromechanics
Exhibition Hall ⊞

Weizikeng

College of Aeronautics ⊛

Beijing Medical University
⊛

Xueyuan Rd.

No. 3 Hospital,
Beijing Medical College
✚

N.

Huayuan

Rd.

A

N

Tayuan

Duyiju

Beijiao

Dewaixiaoguan

Changping Rd.

Huayanli

Huayuan Rd.

E. Huayuan Rd.

☼ Television Factory

Jimenyancun

Huangtingzi

Madian

Jimen ⋔

Hongmiaocun

Xicun

Beitaipingzhuang
Beijing Light Industrial
Products Trade Fairs Hall

College
re

Rd.

★ State Patent Bureau

Auditorium of Newsreel
Film Studio
☒ Yuanwanglou

CAAC Ticket Office

Madianqiao

Jimenqiao

● Beijing Film Studio

News Film Studio ●

⊛ Fanyang

Deshang

M.

Beisanhuan

Rd.

Academy of Sciences
(Min. Com.)

Beitaipingzhuang Supermarket ●

Xinjiekouwai St.

SHUANGXIUYUAN

Xintengbei St.

Beijiao

Beitaipingzhuang Store

Political Science &
w College of China ⊛

Deshengmenwai St.

D

BEITAIPINGZHUANG

Beijiao Bus
Terminal

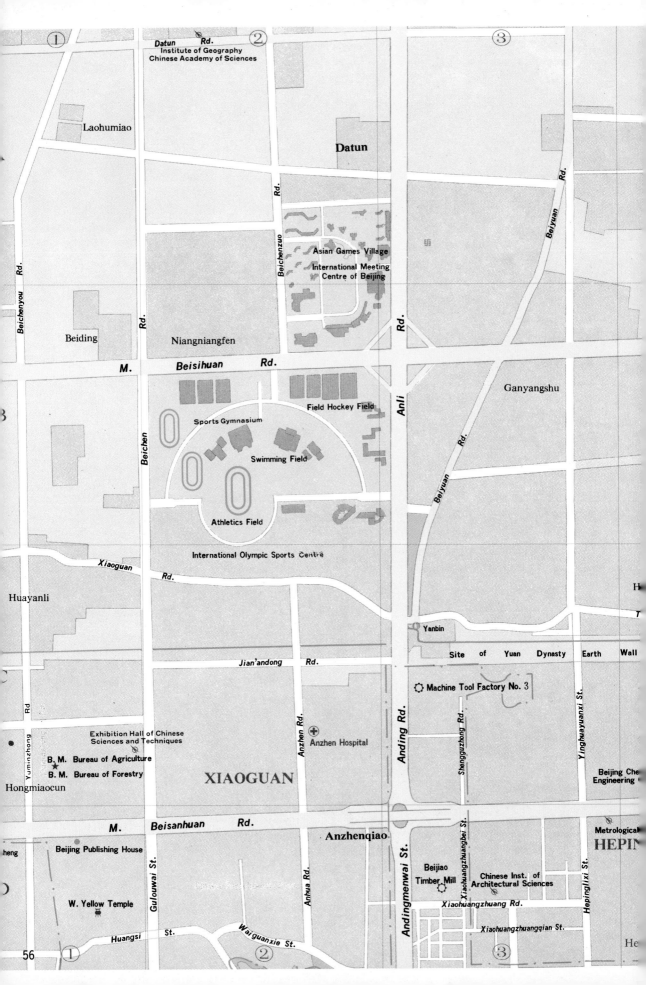

Datun Rd.
Institute of Geography
Chinese Academy of Sciences

Laohumiao

Datun

Beichenzuo Rd.

Asian Games Village

International Meeting
Centre of Beijing

Beiyuan Rd.

Beichenyou Rd.

Beiding

Rd.

Niangniangfen

B

M. **Beisihuan Rd.**

Ganyangshu

Field Hockey Field

Beichen

Sports Gymnasium

Anli Rd.

Swimming Field

Beiyuan Rd.

Athletics Field

International Olympic Sports Centre

Xiaoguan Rd.

Huayanli

H

T

Yanbin

Site of Yuan Dynasty Earth Wall

Jian'andong Rd.

Machine Tool Factory No. 3

Anzhen Rd.

Yuminzhong Rd

Exhibition Hall of Chinese
Sciences and Techniques

Anzhen Hospital

Yinghuayuanxi St.

B. M. Bureau of Agriculture

Shengguizhong Rd.

B. M. Bureau of Forestry

XIAOGUAN

Beijing Che
Engineering

Hongmiaocun

M. **Beisanhuan Rd.**

Anzhenqiao

Metrological

cheng

Beijing Publishing House

Gulouwai St.

Anhua Rd.

Andingmenwai St.

Beijiao
Timber Mill

Xiaohuangzhuangbei St.

Chinese Inst. of
Architectural Sciences

Hepinglixi St.

HEPIN

W. Yellow Temple

Xiaohuangzhuang Rd.

Huangsi St.

Waiguanxie St.

Xiaohuangzhuangqian St.

He

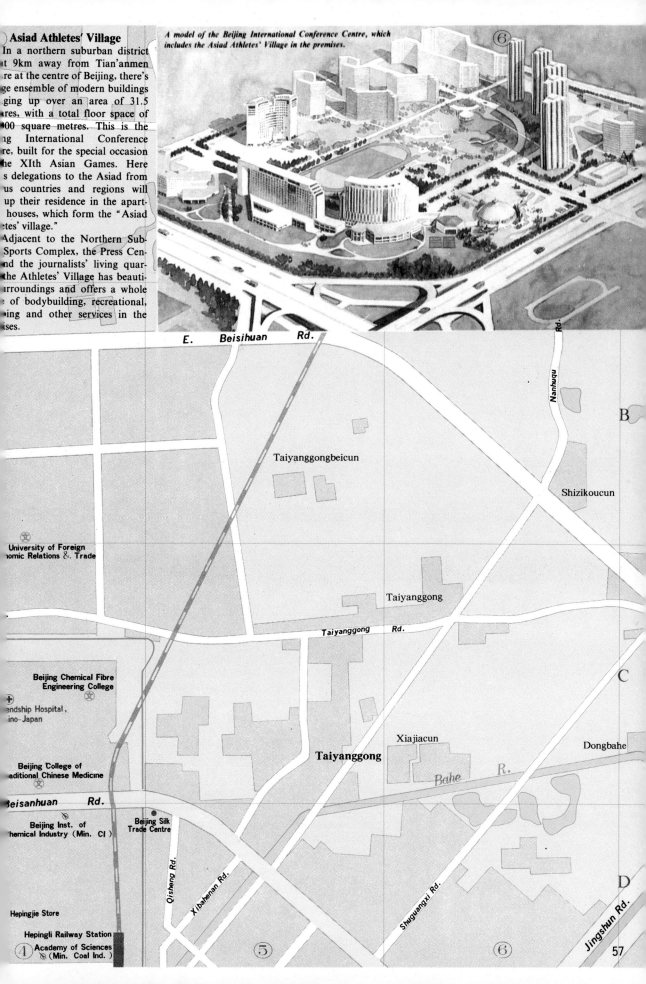

Asiad Athletes' Village

In a northern suburban district t 9km away from Tian'anmen re at the centre of Beijing, there's ge ensemble of modern buildings ging up over an area of 31.5 res, with a total floor space of 00 square metres. This is the ng International Conference re, built for the special occasion the XIth Asian Games. Here s delegations to the Asiad from us countries and regions will up their residence in the apart- houses, which form the "Asiad tes' village."

Adjacent to the Northern Sub- Sports Complex, the Press Cen- nd the journalists' living quar- the Athletes' Village has beauti- rroundings and offers a whole e of bodybuilding, recreational, ing and other services in the ses.

A model of the Beijing International Conference Centre, which includes the Asiad Athletes' Village in the premises.

E. Beisihuan Rd.

Nanhugu Rd.

Taiyanggongbeicun

Shizikoucun

University of Foreign nomic Relations & Trade

Taiyanggong

Taiyanggong Rd.

Beijing Chemical Fibre Engineering College

endship Hospital, ino-Japan

Xiajiacun

Dongbahe

Taiyanggong

Bahe R.

Beijing College of aditional Chinese Medicine

Beisanhuan Rd.

Beijing Inst. of hemical Industry (Min. Cl)

Beijing Silk Trade Centre

Qisheng Rd.

Xibahenan Rd.

Shuguangxi Rd.

Jingshun Rd.

Hepingjie Store

Hepingli Railway Station
Academy of Sciences
(Min. Coal Ind.)

57

Agriculture Film Studio

Polytechnic University

Chinese Academy of Agricultural Sciences

Beixiaguan

B. M. Country & Town Enterprises Administration

Central Colle Finance & Mo

Gigarette Facto

S.

Weigongcun Rd.

Science Universalization Press

Iron & Steel Central Research Inst.

Scientific Research Inst. (Min. R.)

Beijing Institute of Foreign Languages

Weigongcun

H A I

Beijing Stomatological Hospital

BEIXIAGUAN

Baishiqiao

Fahuasi

Central College of Nationalities

Gaoliangqiao Rd.

University of C

China Theatre

ZIZHUYUAN

Wannianqing

State Bureau of Meteorology

Longevity Temple

China Contemporary Literature House

Baishiqiao

Wuta Temple

Touduicun

Nanchang R.

ZIZHUYUAN PARK

Zizhuyuan

National Library of China

Olympic Hotel

BEIJING ZOO

China Electrical Engineering Equipment Corp.

Zizhuyuan

Capital Gymnasium

Beizhan Theatre

Moscow Restaurant

Beijing Exhibition C

Rd.

B. M. Bureau of Gardens

Beijing Movie Theatre

St.

Xizhimenwai

Beijing Computer College

Panzhuang

Xiyuan Hotel

Erligou

Beijing Science & Technology Press

Beijing Planetarium

Xijiao Store

Xizhimenwainan

Rd.

N.

Xisanhuan

Negotiation Building

China Machinery I/E Corp.

China Technical Import Corp.

China Overseas Trading Transport Corp.

China Hardware Minerals I/E Corp.

China Instruments I/E Corp.

Beijing Main Inst. of Mining & Metallurgy

Wenxing St.

Water Resources & Electric Power Publishing House

Beijing College of Arch

Guoyi Hotel

Wenxingdong St.

Zhanlanlu

China International Bookstore

China International Book Trading Corp.

Foreign Language Printing House

Beijing Automobile Plant No. 2

Chinese Architectural Technology Development Center

Rd.

China Pictorial

Dadu

W. Chegongzhuang Rd.

Chegongzhuang

Water Conservation & Hydroelectric Sciences Inst.

B. M. Bureau of Environmental Protection

Urban, Planning Design Inst., Chinese

B. M. Bureau of Tax

B. M. Bureau of Finance

Huayuancun

Ministry of Rural Construction

National Bureau of Surveying and Mapping

Zhanlanguan

GANJIAKOU

Ziyu

State Bureau of Building Material Industry

Chinese Architectural Technology Development Center Exhibition Hall

Auditorium of Architecture

Ganjiakou

Foreign Languages Publishing & Distributing Bureau

Baiwan

Zhuangbei St.

X

Normal College, Beijing

Engineering & Transport College

Baiwanzhuangxi

Rd.

Ganjiakou Food Store

Ganjiakou Store

Chinese Academy of Geology

Baiwanzhuang

Foreign Languages Press

Kouzhonghutong

Mashenmiao

Machine-Building Industry Publishing House

Nanluyuanhutong

Beijing College of Commerce

Scientific Research Inst. (Min. LI)

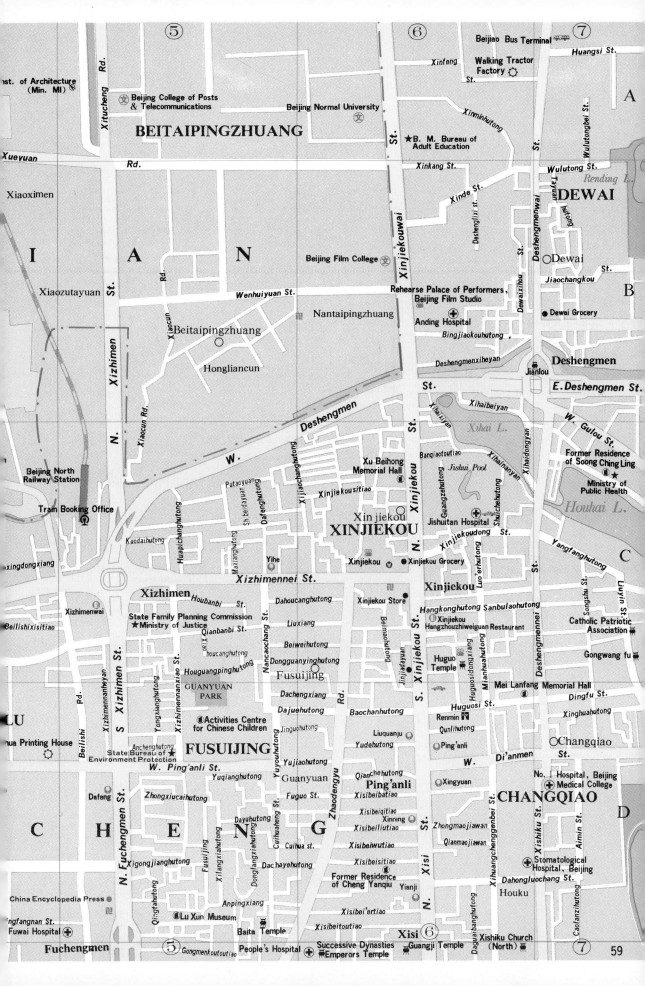

Inst. of Architecture
(Min. MI)

Xitucheng Rd.

Beijing College of Posts
& Telecommunications

Xinfeng St.

Beijiao Bus Terminal

Walking Tractor
Factory

Huangsi St.

A

Beijing Normal University

Xinminhutong

Wulutongbei St.

BEITAIPINGZHUANG

Xueyuan Rd.

St.

B. M. Bureau of
Adult Education

Xinkang St.

Wulutong St.

Tayan

Rending L.

DEWAI

Xiaoximen

Xinde St.

Deshenglixi st.

Dewaixihou

Deshengmenwai

Dewai

I A N

Xizhimen St.

Rd.

Beijing Film College

Xinjiekouwai St.

Jiaochangkou

St.

B

Xiaozutayuan St.

Wenhuiyuan St.

Rehearse Palace of Performers,
Beijing Film Studio

Dewaixihou

Dewai Grocery

Xiaocun

Nantaipingzhuang

Anding Hospital

Bingjiaokouhutong

Xiaocun Rd.

Beitaipingzhuang

Hongliancun

Deshengmenxiheyan

Deshengmenxiheyan

Jianlou

Deshengmen

N.

Deshengmen St.

E. Deshengmen St.

W.

Xihaixiyan

Xihaibeiyan

Xihai L.

W. Gulou St.

Beijing North
Railway Station

Putaoyuan

Deshengmen

St.

Banqiaotoutiao

Jishan Pool

Guangzahutong

Xihainanyan

Xihaidongyan

Former Residence
of Soong Ching Ling

Ministry of
Public Health

Train Booking Office

Xijiaochanghutong

Dafenghutong

Xu Beihong
Memorial Hall

Xinjiekousitiao

Xinjiekou

Shichehutong

Houhai L.

Kuodaihutong

Huapichanghutong

Maxianghutong

Xinjiekoudong St.

Jishuitan Hospital

Xin jiekou
XINJIEKOU

Xinjiekoudong St.

Luo'erhutong

Yangfanghutong

C

xingdongxiang

Yihe

Xinjiekou

Xinjiekou Grocery

N.

Xinjiekou

Xinjiekou

Songshu St.

Liuyin St.

Xizhimennei St.

Xinjiekou Store

Hangkonghutong Sanbulaohutong

Catholic Patriotic
Association

Xizhimen

Houbanbi St.

Dahoucanghutong

Xinjiekou
Hangzhouzhiweiguan Restaurant

Beimaohutong

Xinjiekou St.

Gongwang fu

State Family Planning Commission
Ministry of Justice

Qianbanbi St.

Liuxiang

Huguosidongxiang

Mianhuahutong

Deshengmennei

Xizhimenwai

Xizhimenheyan

Xizhimennanxiao St.

zhoucanghutong

Beiweihutong

Dongguanyinghutong

Huguo
Temple

Mei Lanfang Memorial Hall

Beilishixisitiao

Houguangpinghutong

Fusuijing

Jinjiadayuan

Huguosi

Dingfu St.

Renmin

Xinghuahutong

LU

**GUANYUAN
PARK**

Dachengxiang

Baochanhutong

Qunlihutong

Changqiao

Activities Centre
for Chinese Children

Dajuehutong

Liuquanju

Ping'anli

St.

ua Printing House

Jinguohutong

Yudehutong

Xingyuan

No. I Hospital, Beijing
Medical College

State Bureau of
Environment Protection

Anchenghutong

FUSUIJING

W. Ping'anli St.

Yujiaohutong

Qianchehutong

Di'anmen

W.

CHANGQIAO

Dafeng

Yuqianghutong

Guanyuan

Ping'anli

Zhongmaojiawan

Xishiku St.

Zhongxiucaihutong

Fuguo St.

Xisibeibatiao

Qianmaojiawan

Stomatological
Hospital, Beijing

C H E N

Dayuhutong

Xilangxiahutong

Cuihuaheng St.

Cuihua st.

Xisibeiqitiao

Xinning

Xisibeiliutiao

G

Xisibeiwutiao

Xihuangchenggenbei St.

Houku

Xigongjianghutong

Fusuijing

Donglangxiahutong

Dachayehutong

Xisibeisitiao

Xisi

Dahongluochang St.

China Encyclopedia Press

Qingtahutong

Anpingxiang

Former Residence
of Cheng Yanqiu

Yianji

N.

ngfannan St.

Fuwai Hospital

Lu Xun Museum

Baita Temple

Xisibei'ertiao

Fuchengmen

⑤ Gongmenkoutoutiao

People's Hospital

Xisibeitoutiao

Successive Dynasties
Emperors Temple

Xisi ⑥

Guangji Temple

Xishiku Church
(North)

⑦

Daguaibanghutong

Caolanzihutong

59

① ② ③

Beijing College of Light Industry

Fucheng Rd.

○ Ganjiakou

GANJIAKOU

Dongdiaoyutai

● China Electronic-Devices Industry Corp.

SOONG CHING LING CHILDREN'S SCIENCE PARK

Diaoyutai State Guesthouse

Auditorium of Goods & Materials Administration

Ministry of Goods & Materials ★

Sanlihe Rd.

N. Yuetan St.

Hongta Auditorium

Yuyuan L. (Deep Jade Pool)

Guiyang Hotel

Jinghu Food Store

Sanlihebei St.

S. Yuetan St

Liulinguan

Water Conservation & Hydroelectric Sciences Inst.

Ministry of Commission Electronics Industry

State Planning ★ State Bureau of Statistics ★ Ministry of Finance

Auditorium of Machine Building & Electronic Industry

Sanlihe Store

Workers' Club, Xicheng

HAI DIAN

Chinese Academy of Sciences

Auditorium of Chinese Academy of Sciences ★

State Science & Technology Commission

State Science & Technology Association

YUETAN

Central Colour Television Centre

Military Museum of the Chinese People's Revolution

Yanjing Hotel

China Information Insititute of Science and Technology

B Gongzhufen

Fuxing Ave.

Scientific and Technical Exchange Centre

Fuxingmenwai

Booking Office, Civil Aviation of China

Jingxi Hotel

Beijing General Inst. of Nonferrous Metallurgy Design.

★ Ministry of Communications

Beijing Railway Bureau ★

Muxidi

China Machine & Equipment I/E Corp.

All-Chi Federa Trade

Fuxing Hospital

Yangfangdianxi Rd.

YANGFANGDIAN

B. M. Institute of Surveying Mapping ★

○ Yangfangdian

Yangfangdian Rd.

Beifengwo Rd.

Beijing Public Security University

Baiyun Rd.

Baiyunguan ☵ Ta Baiyun

Beijing General Railway Hospital ✚

Beifengwo Store ●

Club of Railway Bureau

C

E. Lianhuachi Rd.

Electro Factor

Xibianmen Railway Station

Nanfengwo

LIANHUACHI PARK

Maliandaobei Rd.

Beijing Steel Works

Shoupakouxi St.

Xiaomachanghali

Xiaomachangxixiang

Shoupakoubei St.

Ten

Lianhua (Lotus) Pond

Metallurgical Machinery Plant ☼

Mining Machinery Plant ☼

Lianhuahehutong

Louwailou

X

Tiann

Forklift Factory (Main)

○ Guangwai

Guang'anmenwai St.

FENGTAI

Maliandao

Lianhua R.

GUANGWAI

Hongjudong St.

Shoupakounan St.

D

Guang'an Rd.

Wanzi St.

Maliandao Rd.

Maliandaobei St.

Hongtian Rd.

Hongjiuerxiang

Machine Tools Factory No. 2

Lianhuachi Bus Terminal

Maliandaozhong St.

62

② ③

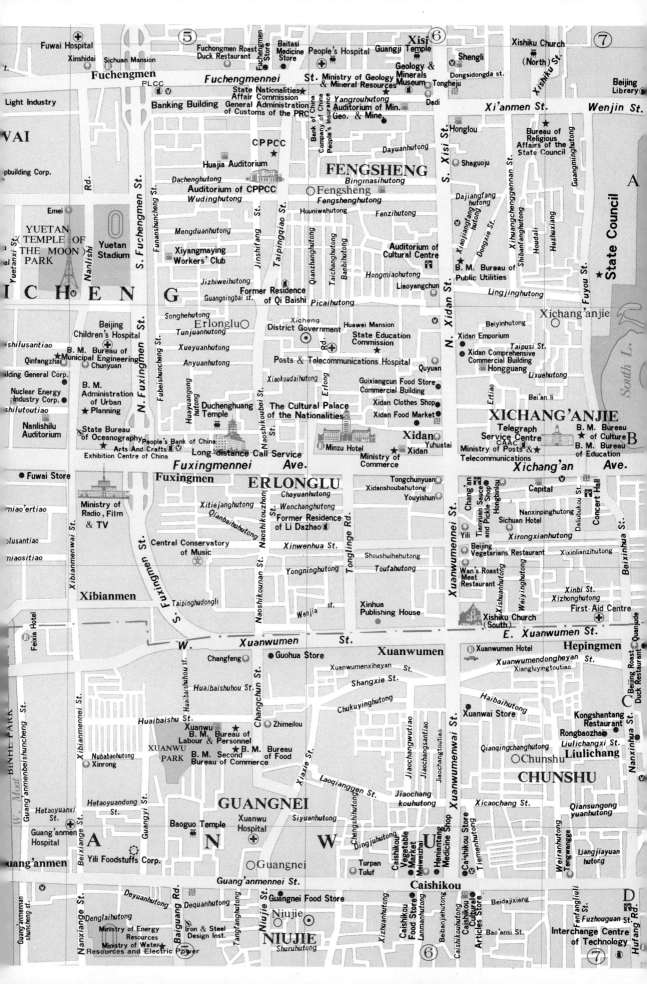

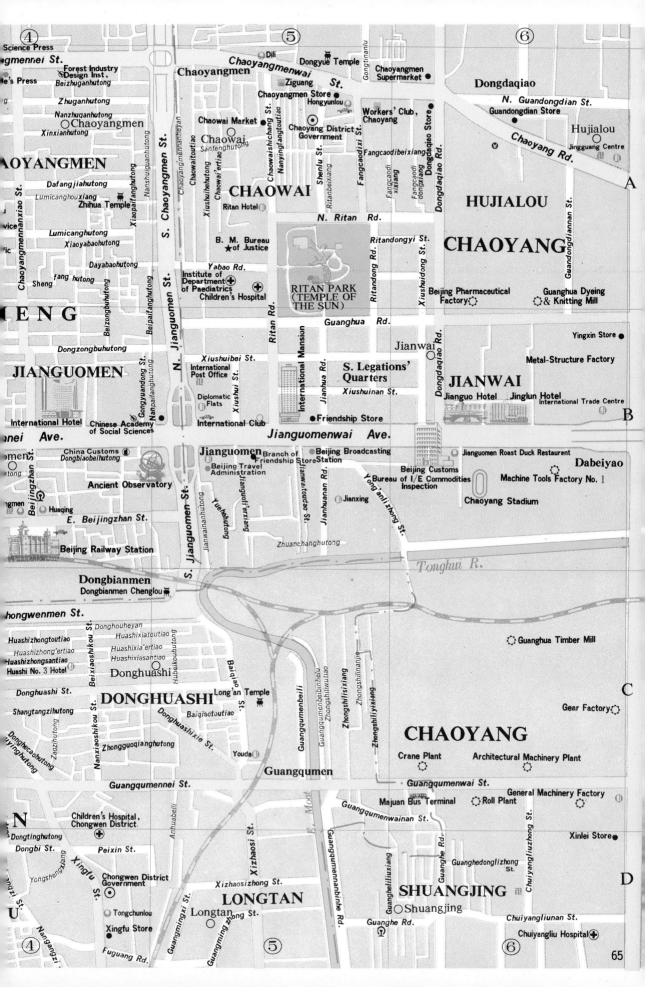

Science Press

gmennei St.

Forest Industry
Design Inst,
Beizhuganhutong

le's Press

Zhuganhutong

Nanzhuganhutong

○ Chaoyangmen

Xinxianhutong

AOYANGMEN

Dafangjiahutong

Lumicanghouxiang

Zhihua Temple

vice

Lumicanghutong

Xiaoyabaohutong

Dayabaohutong

Sheng fang hutong

ENG

Dongzongbuhutong

JIANGUOMEN

Dili

Chaoyangmenwai St.

Dongyue Temple

Gongtinanlu

Chaoyangmen

Ziguang

Chaoyangmen Store

Hongyunlou

Chaoyangmen
Supermarket

Dongdaqiao

N. Guandongdian St.

Guandongdian Store

Chaowai Market

Chaowaishichang St.

Chaowai

Sanfenghutong

Chaowaitoutiao

Chaowaierduo

Xiushuikehutong

Chaowai'ertiao

Ritan Hotel

CHAOWAI

Shenlu St.

Ritanbeixiang

Workers' Club,
Chaoyang

Chaoyang District
Government

Fangcaodixi St.

Fangcaodibeixiang

Fangcaodixixiang

Fangcaodidongxiang

Dongdaqiao Store

Dongdaqiao Rd.

Chaoyang Rd.

Hujialou

Jingguang Centre

A

HUJIALOU

CHAOYANG

Guandongdiannan St.

N. Ritan Rd.

B. M. Bureau
★ of Justice

Yabao Rd.

Institute of
Department
of Paediatrics
Children's Hospital

Ritan Rd.

RITAN PARK
(TEMPLE OF
THE SUN)

Ritandongyi St.

Ritandong Rd.

Xiushuidong St.

Beijing Pharmaceutical
Factory

Guanghua Dyeing
& Knitting Mill

Guanghua Rd.

Jianwai

Yingxin Store

Metal-Structure Factory

Xiushuibei St.

International
Post Office

Xiushui St.

International Mansion

Jianhua Rd.

S. Legations'
Quarters

Dongdaqiao Rd.

JIANWAI

Diplomatic
Flats

International Hotel

Chinese Academy
of Social Sciences

Gongyuandong St.

Nanpaifanghutong

Xiushui St.

Xiushuinan St.

Friendship Store

International Club

Jianguo Hotel

Jinglun Hotel

International Trade Centre

B

nei Ave.

Ave.

Jianguomenwai Ave.

China Customs
Dongbiaobeihutong

Beijingzhan St.

tong

Jianguomen

Branch of
Friendship Store

Beijing Travel
Administration

Jianguotou St.

Jianguomenanhutong

Yuehehutong

Beijing Broadcasting
Station

Jianwaitoudao St.

Jianhuanan Rd.

Jianxing

Yong'anlizhong St.

Beijing Customs
Bureau of I/E Commodities
Inspection

Jianguomen Roast Duck Restaurant

Chaoyang Stadium

Machine Tools Factory No. 1

Dabeiyao

Ancient Observatory

Huaqing

E. Beijingzhan St.

Zhuanchanghutong

Tonghui R.

Beijing Railway Station

Dongbianmen

Dongbianmen Chenglou

hongwenmen St.

Huashizhongtoutiao

Huashizhong'ertiao

Huashizhongsantiao

Huashi No. 3 Hotel

Beixiaoshikou St.

Donghouheyan

Huashixiatoutiao

Huashixia'ertiao

Huashixiasantiao

Hubeikouhutong

Donghuashi

Guanghua Timber Mill

Zhongshilisixiang

Zhongshilinanjie

Zhongshilisanxiang

Zhongshiliyixiang

C

Donghuashi St.

Shangtangzihutong

DONGHUASHI

Long'an Temple

Baiqiao Rd.

Baiqiaotoutiao

Donghuashixie St.

Gear Factory

Dongchecaohutong

yinghutong

Zaozihutong

Nanxiaoshikou St.

Zhongguoqianghutong

Youda

CHAOYANG

Crane Plant

Architectural Machinery Plant

Guangqumen

Guangqumennei St.

Guangqumenbeili

Guangqumenbeibinhelu

Zhongshiliwuliao

Guangqumenwai St.

General Machinery Factory

N

Children's Hospital,
Chongwen District

Dongtinghutong

Dongbi St.

Peixin St.

Anhuabeili

E. Moat

Majuan Bus Terminal

Guangqumennan Rd.

Roll Plant

Guangqumennainan St.

Chuiyangliuzhong St.

Xinlei Store

D

U

Yongshengxiang

Nangangzi

Xingfu St.

Chongwen District
Government

Tongchunlou

Xingfu Store

Xizhaosi St.

Xizhaosizhong St.

LONGTAN

Longtan

Guangmingxi St.

Guangming zhong St.

Guangming St.

Fuguang Rd.

Guangheliliuxiang

Guanghe Rd.

SHUANGJING

Shuangjing

Guanghedonglizhong St.

Guanghe Rd.

Chuiyangliunan St.

Chuiyangliu Hospital

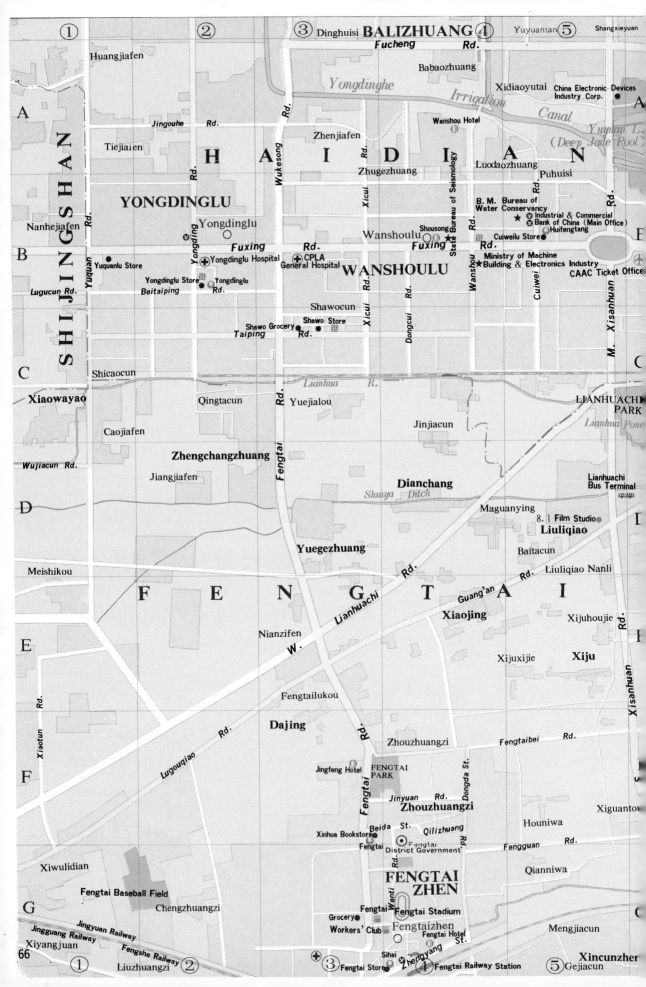

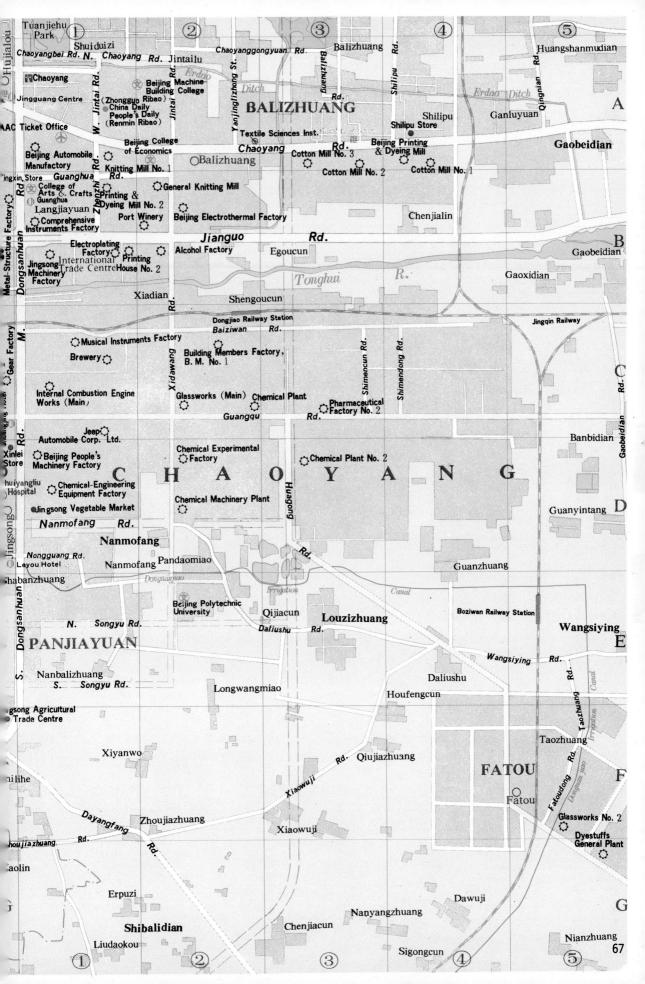

Tuanjiehu
Park
Shuiduizi
② ③ Balizhuang ④ ⑤
Huangshanmudian
Chaoyangbei Rd. N. Chaoyang Rd. Jintailu
Chaoyanggongyuan Rd. Balizhuang Rd.
Chaoyang
Jingguang Centre
Beijing Machine
Building College
Erdao Ditch
Shilipu
Erdao Ditch
Qingnian Rd.
A
(Zhongguo Ribao)
China Daily
People's Daily
(Renmin Ribao)
Shilipu
Ganluyuan
CAAC Ticket Office
Beijing College
of Economics
Textile Sciences Inst.
Shilipu Store
Gaobeidian
Chaoyang Rd.
Beijing Printing
& Dyeing Mill
Beijing Automobile
Manufactory
Knitting Mill No. 1
Balizhuang
Cotton Mill No. 3
Cotton Mill No. 2
Cotton Mill No. 1
Jingxin Store Guanghua Rd.
College of
Arts & Crafts
Guanghua
General Knitting Mill
Printing &
Dyeing Mill No. 2
Port Winery
Beijing Electrothermal Factory
Chenjialin
Langjiayuan
Comprehensive
Instruments Factory
Jianguo Rd.
Gaobeidian
Metal-Structure Factory
Electroplating
Factory
Printing
House No. 2
Alcohol Factory
Egoucun
Gaoxidian
Dongsanhuan Rd.
Jingsong
Machinery
Factory
International
Trade Centre
Xiadian
Shengoucun
Tonghui R.
Gear Factory
Dongjiao Railway Station
Baiziwan Rd.
Jingqin Railway
Musical Instruments Factory
Building Members Factory,
B. M. No. 1
Shimencun Rd.
Shimendong Rd.
C
Brewery
Xidawang Rd.
Internal Combustion Engine
Works (Main)
Glassworks (Main)
Chemical Plant
Guangqu Rd.
Pharmaceutical
Factory No. 2
Jeep
Automobile Corp. Ltd.
Chemical Experimental
Factory
Chemical Plant No. 2
Banbidian
Gaobeidian Rd.
Xinlei
Store
Beijing People's
Machinery Factory
C H A O Y A N G
Shuiyangliu
Hospital
Chemical-Engineering
Equipment Factory
Chemical Machinery Plant
Guanyintang
D
Jingsong
Jinsong Vegetable Market
Nanmofang Rd.
Huagong Rd.
Nanmofang
Nongguang Rd.
Layou Hotel
Nanmofang
Pandaomiao
Guanzhuang
Shabanzhuang
Dongmiaoqiao
Irrigation
Canal
Boziwan Railway Station
Wangsiying
E
Beijing Polytechnic
University
Qijiacun
Louzizhuang
Dongsanhuan Rd. N.
N. Songyu Rd.
Daliushu
Wangsiying Rd.
PANJIAYUAN
Daliushu
Taozhuang Rd.
Canal
Nanbalizhuang
S. Songyu Rd.
Longwangmiao
Houfengcun
Taozhuang
S. Dongsanhuan Rd.
Jingsong Agricultural
Trade Centre
Xiyanwo
Qiujiazhuang
Fatoudong Rd.
Dongguanjiao Irrigation
Glassworks No. 2
Xiaowuji Rd.
FATOU
F
Bahilihe
Dayangfang Rd.
Zhoujiazhuang
Xiaowuji
Fatou
Dyestuffs
General Plant
Zhoujiazhuang Rd.
Gaolin
Erpuzi
Dawuji
G
Shibalidian
Nanyangzhuang
Nianzhuang
Liudaokou
Chenjiacun
Sigongcun
① ② ③ ④ ⑤

67

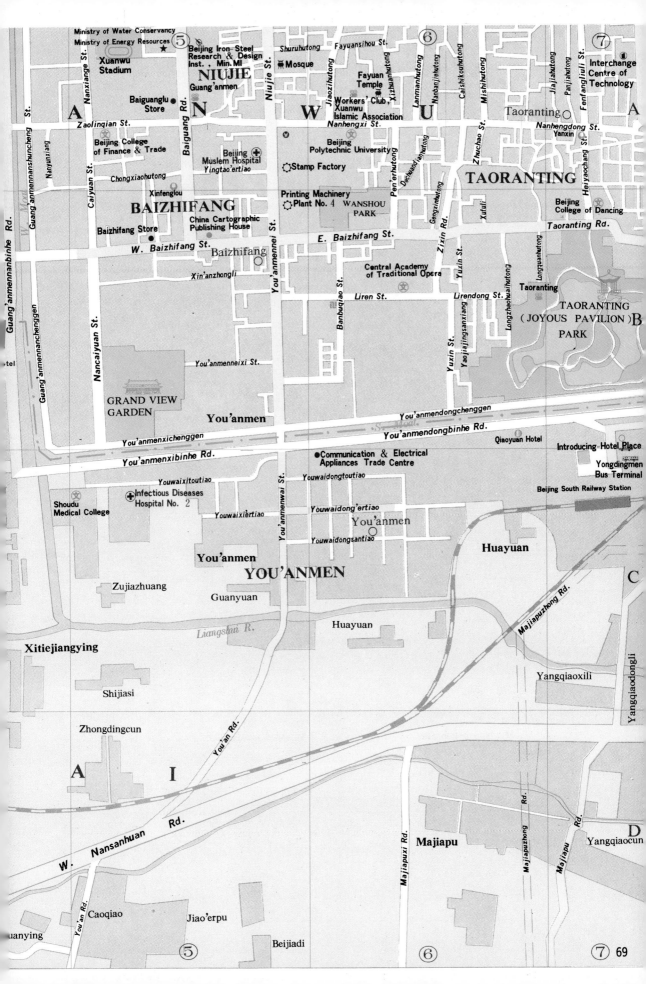

Ministry of Water Conservancy
Ministry of Energy Resources ⑤

Xuanwu
Stadium

★ Beijing Iron-Steel
Research & Design
Inst., Min. MI

NIUJIE

Guang'anmen

Baiguanglu
Store

Zaolinqian St.

Beijing College
of Finance & Trade

Chongxiaohutong

Xinfenglou

BAIZHIFANG

Baizhifang Store

China Cartographic
Publishing House

W. Baizhifang St.

Baizhifang

Xin'anzhongli

You'anmenneixi St.

**GRAND VIEW
GARDEN**

You'anmen

You'anmenxichenggen

You'anmenxibinhe Rd.

Youwaixitoutiao

Shoudu
Medical College

Infectious Diseases
Hospital No. 2

Youwaixiertiao

You'anmen

Zujiazhuang

Guanyuan

YOU'ANMEN

Xitiejiangying

Shijiasi

Zhongdingcun

A I

Nanxiange St.
Nanyunxiang
Caiyuan St.
Guang'anmennanshuncheng
Guang'anmennanchenggen
Guang'anmennanbinhe Rd.
W. Rd.

Baiguang Rd.

Beijing
Muslem Hospital ✚
Yingtao'ertiao

Nancaiyuan St.

Shuruhutong

Niujie St.

Mosque

N W U

Jiaozihutong

Fayuansihou St.

Fayuan
Temple

Workers' Club
Xuanwu
Islamic Association

Nanhengxi St.

Beijing
Polytechnic University

Stamp Factory

Printing Machinery
Plant No. 4

WANSHOU
PARK

E. Baizhifang St.

Banbuqiao St.

Central Academy
of Traditional Opera

Liren St.

You'anmennei St.

You'anmen

You'anmendongchenggen

You'anmendongbinhe Rd.

S. Moat

Communication & Electrical
Appliances Trade Centre

Youwaidongtoutiao

You'anmenwai St.

Youwaidong'ertiao

You'anmen

Youwaidongsantiao

Huayuan

Liangshan R.

Huayuan

You'an Rd.

W. Nansanhuan Rd.

You'an Rd.

Caoqiao

Jiao'erpu

Beijiadi

Xizhuanhutong
Dachengdianhutong
Pen'erhutong
Gengzihutong
Zixin Rd.
Yuxin St.
Yuxin St.
Yaojiajingsanxiang
Lirendong St.
Longzhaohutong

Lannanhutong
Nanbanjiehutong
Caishikouhutong

Zhuchao St.

Xufuli

Taoranting

Longhuahutong

TAORANTING

Beijing
College of Dancing

Taoranting Rd.

Taoranting

**TAORANTING
(JOYOUS PAVILION)
PARK**

Qiaoyuan Hotel

Introducing-Hotel Place

Yongdingmen
Bus Terminal

Beijing South Railway Station

Majiapuzhong Rd.

Yangqiaoxili

Majiapuxi Rd.

Majiapudong Rd.

Majiapu Rd.

Yangqiaodongli

Majiapu

Yangqiaocun

Mishihutong
Heiyaochang St.
Fenfangliuli St.
Jiajiahutong
Panjiahutong

⑦

Interchange
Centre of
Technology

Taoranting

Nanhengdong St.
Yanxin

A

B

C D

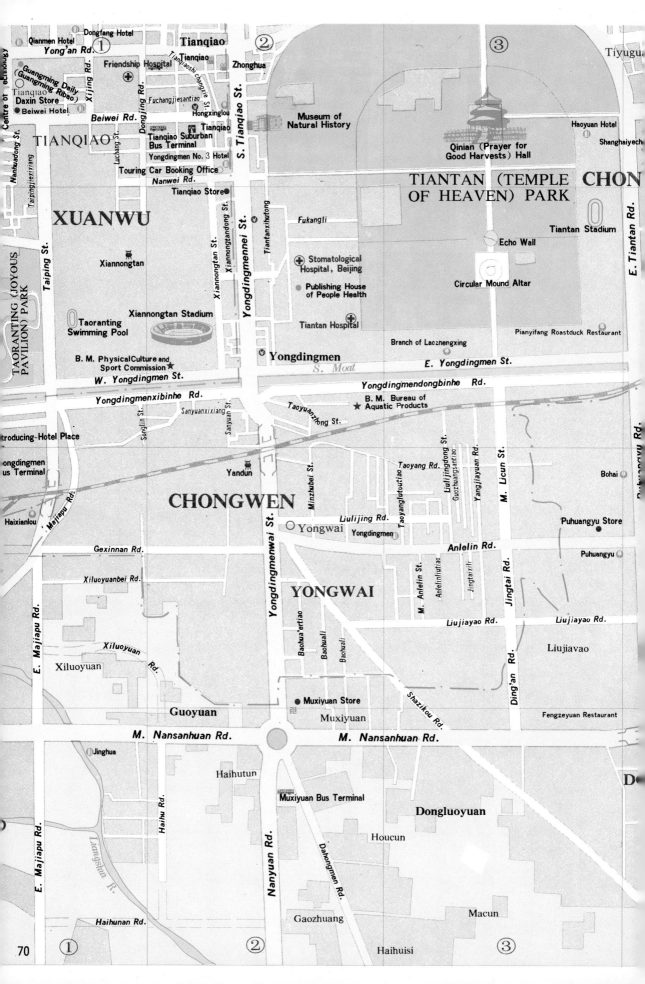

Qianmen Hotel
Dongfang Hotel
Yong'an Rd. ①
Tianqiao ②
③
Tiyugu

Tianqiao
Tianqiaoshi changjie St.
Zhonghua

Guangming Daily
(Guangming Ribao)
Friendship Hospital
Tianqiao
Daxin Store
Beiwei Hotel

Fuchangjiesantiao

Hongxinglou
Museum of
Natural History

Qinian (Prayer for
Good Harvests) Hall

Haoyuan Hotel
Shanghaiyech

Beiwei Rd.
Tianqiao
Tianqiao Suburban
Bus Terminal
Yongdingmen No. 3 Hotel
Touring Car Booking Office

TIANQIAO

Nanhuadong St.
Taipingjiexixiang

Luchang St.
Dongjing Rd.

Nanwei Rd.
Tianqiao Store

XUANWU

**TIANTAN (TEMPLE CHON
OF HEAVEN) PARK**

S. Tianqiao St.

Xiannongtandong St.
Xiannongtan St.
Yongdingmennei St.
Tiantanxihutong

Fukangli

Tiantan Stadium

Xiannongtan

Stomatological
Hospital, Beijing

Echo Wall

TAORANTING (JOYOUS PAVILION) PARK
Taiping St.

Xiannongtan Stadium
Taoranting
Swimming Pool

Publishing House
of People Health

Circular Mound Altar

B. M. PhysicalCulture and
Sport Commission ★

Tiantan Hospital

Pianyifang Roastduck Restaurant

W. Yongdingmen St.
Yongdingmen

Branch of Laoznengxing

E. Tiantan Rd.

S. Moat
E. Yongdingmen St.

Yongdingmenxibinhe Rd.

Yongdingmendongbinhe Rd.

Sanglin St.
Sanyuanxixiang
Sanyuan St.

Taoyuanzhong St.
B. M. Bureau of
Aquatic Products ★

troducing-Hotel Place

Yandun
Minzhubei St.

Taoyang Rd.
Liulijingdong St.
Guozhuangsantiao
Yangjiayuan Rd.
M. Licun St.
Bohai

ongdingmen
us Terminal

CHONGWEN

Taoyanglutoutiao

Haixianlou

Majiapu Rd.

Yongwai

Liulijing Rd.
Yongdingmen

Puhuangyu Store

Anlelin Rd.

Puhuangyu

Gexinnan Rd.

Yongdingmenwai St.

M. Anlelin St.
Anlelinlitiao
Jingtaerxih

Jingtai Rd.

Xiluoyuanbei Rd.

YONGWAI

Liujiayao Rd.
Liujiayao Rd.

E. Majiapu Rd.
Xiluoyuan Rd.
Xiluoyuan

Baohua'ertiao
Baohuali
Baohuali

Liujiayao

Ding'an Rd.

Guoyuan

Muxiyuan Store

Shazikou Rd.

Fengzeyuan Restaurant

M. Nansanhuan Rd.
Muxiyuan

M. Nansanhuan Rd.

Jinghua
Haihutun

Nanyuan Rd.

Muxiyuan Bus Terminal

Dongluoyuan

Houcun

Dahongmen Rd.

Liangshan R.

Macun

Haihunan Rd.
Gaozhuang

Haihuisi

YUGUANLU
Xingfu Store
Fuguang

Guangming Store

Chuiyangliu Hospital
Jingsong

China Sports Federation★
State Physical Culture and Sports Commission
Guangmingxi St.
Guangmingzhong St.
E. Guanghe St.
Jingsongxi St.
Jingsongzhong St.
Jingsongdongkou St.

Guangming Rd.
Jingsong Rd.
JINGSONG

yuan Rd.
Xingluda St.
Jingsong Store

Beijing Gymnasium
Jingsong Hotel
Dadu Restaurant
Jingsong
S. Jingsong Rd.

Longtan Rd.
Longtan Rd.
Guangqumennanbinhe Rd.
Leyou

Longtanli
Yuandushi Temple
LONGTAN PARK
B. Moat
E. Panjiayuan Rd.
A

Longtan L.
Panjiayuan
Huawei Rd.

ute Tower
Zuo'anmennei St.
BEIJING AMUSEMENT PARK
Panjiayuan Rd.
Nanjiasong
PANJIAYUAN
B

S. Dongsanhuan Rd.
CHAOYANG

Moat
Zuo'anmenxibinhe Rd.
Zuo'anmendongbinhe Rd.
Tumour Hospital

Zuo'anmen
Zuo'an Rd.

Fangcheng Rd.
Fangzhuang Rd.
Balihe
Jingsong Agricultural Trade Centre

Fangqun Rd.
Fanggu Rd.
Fangxing Rd.

Pufang Rd.
Pufang Rd.
C
Shilihe

Puhuangyu
Daliushu

Qunxing Rd.
ENGTAI
E. Nansanhuan Rd.
E. Nansanhuan Rd.
Zhoujiazhuang Rd.

Fangjiazhuang
Fenzhongsi
Zaolin

angying Club
ongtiejiangying
ANGYING
Dongtiejiangyinghengtoutiao

Dongtiejiangyingshunsitiao
Songzhuang
Chengshousi
Xiaohongmen Rd.
D

Guanjiakeng

Rd.
Yuejincun

Longzhaoshu

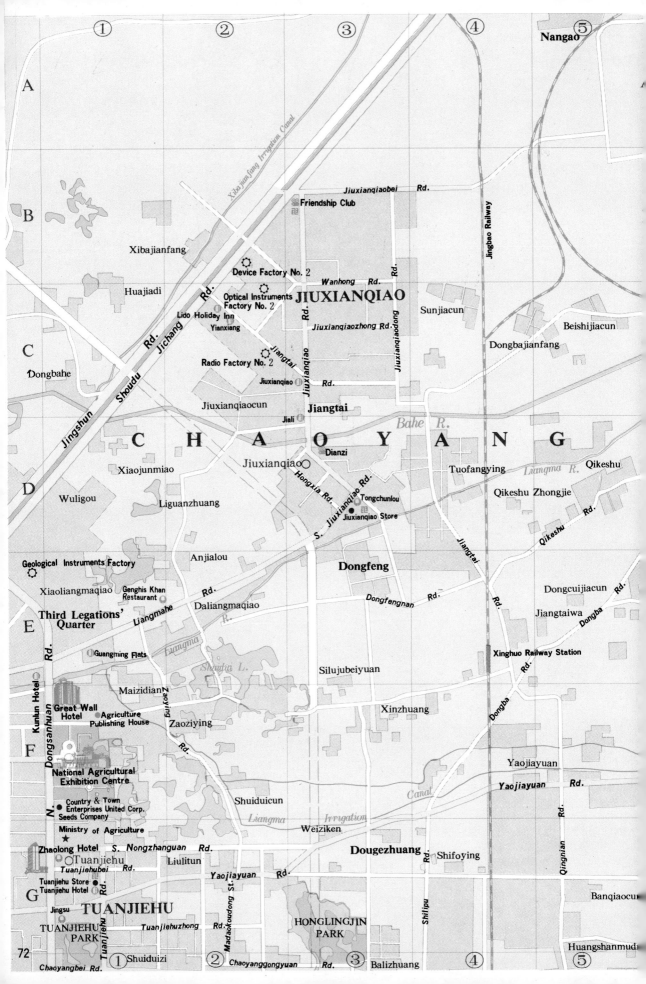

Nangao

A

B

Xiajianfang Irrigation Canal

Jiuxianqiaobei　Rd.

Friendship Club

Xibajianfang

Device Factory No. 2

Wanhong　Rd.

JIUXIANQIAO

Huajiadi

Optical Instruments
Factory No. 2

Lido Holiday Inn

Yianxiang

Jiuxianqiaozhong Rd.

Sunjiacun

Beishijiacun

Dongbajianfang

C

Dongbahe

Jiangtai

Radio Factory No. 2

Jiuxianqiao

Jiuxianqiaocun

Jiangtai

Jiali

Jiuxianqiao

Bahe R.

Liangma R.

Qikeshu

Xiaojunmiao

Dianzi

Tuofangying

Qikeshu Zhongjie

D

Wuligou

Liguanzhuang

Hongxia Rd.

S. Jiuxianqiao Rd.

Tongchunlou

Jiuxianqiao Store

Qikeshu　Rd.

C　H　A　O　Y　A　N　G

Geological Instruments Factory

Anjialou

Dongfeng

Dongcuijiacun

Xiaoliangmaqiao

Genghis Khan
Restaurant

Rd.

Daliangmaqiao

Dongfengnan　Rd.

Jiangtaiwa

Dongba　Rd.

Third Legations'
Quarter

Liangmahe

*Liangma
R.*

E

Guangming Flats

Shuba L.

Silujubeiyuan

Xinghuo Railway Station

Dongba

Kunlun Hotel

Maizidian

Zaoying

Xinzhuang

Great Wall
Hotel

Agriculture
Publishing House

Zaoziying

Rd.

F

National Agricultural
Exhibition Centre

Country & Town
Enterprises United Corp.
Seeds Company

Shuiduicun

Liangma　*Irrigation*　Canal

Weiziken

Yaojiayuan

Yaojiayuan　Rd.

Ministry of Agriculture

Zhaolong Hotel

S. Nongzhanguan　Rd.

Dougezhuang

Shifoying

Tuanjiehu

Liulitun

Tuanjiehubei
Tuanjiehu Store
Tuanjiehu Hotel

Rd.

Yaojiayuan

Rd.

Banqiaocu

G

Jingsu

TUANJIEHU

Tuanjiehuzhong

HONGLINGJIN
PARK

TUANJIEHU
PARK

Huangshanmud

Chaoyangbei Rd.

Jichang
Rd.

Shoudu

Jingshun

Jiuxianqiaobei
Rd.

Jingbao Railway

Madaokoudong St.

Distribution of Famous Scenic Spots Across China

Throughout China, which lies in the east of the world, there exist mountains and rivers of magnificent or elegant beauty, and natural landscape in many and varied forms. Over the ages, the various nationalities of China joined their efforts to create a shining civilization, leaving behind tens of thousands of historical relics to beautify the country. According to decisions announced by the Chinese Government in 1982 and 1988, there are altogether 84 important national scenic spots in China.

Among those scenic spots are the Lijiang River at Guilin with its unique landscape and blue water, the lofty five mountains well-known since ancient times, the Three Gorges of the Changjiang River, which are at once imposing and elegant, the West Lake at Hangzhou, which boasts a delicate beauty, the magnificent waterfall at Huangguoshu, the Five Lakes area with large stretches of volcanic lava, the Karst Forest at Lunan, the picturesque Mt. Huangshan and the four Buddhist Mountains. All these places make China one of the countries in the world noted for their beautiful landscape.

As a country with an ancient civilization, China has a multitude of historical relics, many of which are known throughout the world. To name a few: the world-famous Great Wall, the Imperial Palace — the largest and best preserved palace complex still in existence in the world, the Dunhuang Grottos — the treasure trove of grotto arts, and the terra-cotta warrior figurine cave at the tomb of the First Emperor of the Qin Dynasty, known as the seventh wonder of the world. All of them can count as precious items of the world's cultural heritage.

10 Famous Scenic Attractions in China Chosen in 1985

No.	Name	Introduction
1	The Great Wall	It begins in the east from the Shanhai Pass and ends at the Jiayu Pass in the west, running through Hebei, Shanxi, Nei Mongol, Shaanxi, Ningxia, and Gansu Provinces (Aut. Reg.) and Beijing. The Great Wall is famous for its Great projecting and magnificent spectacle.
2	The Mountains and Waters in Guilin	The scenery is designated to the mountains and waters along the Lijiang River between Guilin and Yangshuo county, the Guangxi Zhuang Autonomous Region. The scenery is known for its green gills, clear waters, peculiar karst caves and stones and enjoys the reputation of "the finest mountains and waters in the world".
3	Xihu Lake, Hangzhou	The Xihu Lake (the West Lake) is situated to the west of Hangzhou city and is surrounded by mountains on three sides. It is famous for its natural beauty of lakes and mountains and picturesque landscape. As a poem goes: The lake first sparkled in the sun's bright dazzling sheen, Then wonder-making showers the verdant hills would screen. For varied charms the west Lake well may I compare, To Xizi, Who, adorned or not, alike was fair.
4	Palace Museum, Beijing	Located at the center of Beijing, it was the imperial residence of the Ming and Qing dynasties. It is famous for its magnificent buildings and luxurious ornaments. There are rich and varied cultural and artistic treasures in it.
5	Suzhou Gardens	It is designated to the Suzhou proper. The Gardens here are famous for their ingenous designs, attractive rocheries, clean waters, pavilions and halls and natural landscape. A saying goes: The views in the gardens never look the same and even one step makes a difference.
6	The Huangshan Mountain, Anhui	Located in southern Anhui Province, it is a tourist attraction for the four marvels, e.g. fantastic pines, grotesque rocks, the sea of clouds and hot springs, while the lakes, water falls, crooks and pools contend in beauty and fascination.
7	The Three Gorges in the Changjiang River	The Three Gorges — the Qutang Gorge, Wuxia Gorge and Xiling Gorge start Sichuan's Baidicheng in the west and terminate at Hubei's Nanjin Pass in the east. They concentrate sceneries of Mountains and waters together. Each Gorge has its own peculiar scenery. The Qutang Gorge is stately and steep, the Wuxia Gorge is profound and graceful and the Xiling Gorge has many dangerous shoals and rapid currends. With many famous sites, historic monuments and inscriptions embellished in the mountains both side the Gorges. They are so called "Historical Picture Corridor".
8	Riyue Lake, Taiwan	Located in Nantou County, it is the famous scenery in Taiwan. Surrounded by mountains, the lake has an island in its center that divides the water surface into two parts. The northern part is in a round shape like the sun and the southern part looks like a cresceat, its name was so got.
9	Chengde Summer Resort	Surrounded by mountains, it lies in the nouthern part of Hebei province. With magnificent relief and moderate climate, it is the largest existing imperial summer resort in China.
10	Terra-Cotta Warrior and Horse Figures, Xi'an	Located at east to Lintong county town, Shaanxi Province, they are the funeral objects of the first emperor of Qin dynasty. Arranged in mighty combat formations the terra-cotta figures of warriors, horses and chariots are real-sized and extraodinary.

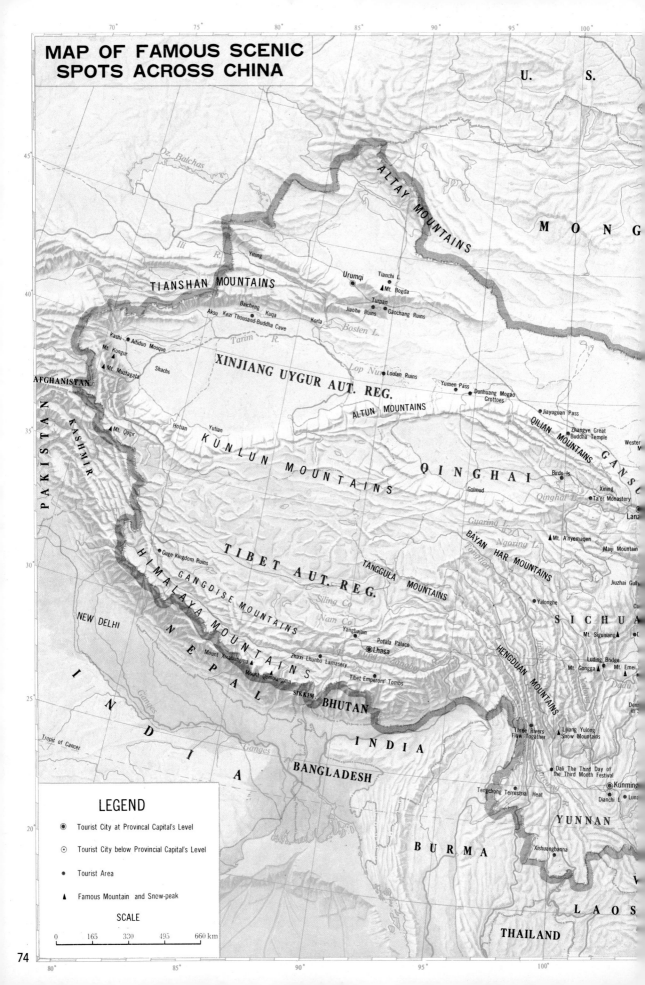

MAP OF FAMOUS SCENIC SPOTS ACROSS CHINA

U. S.

MONG

ALTAY MOUNTAINS

Oz. Balchas

Ili

TIANSHAN MOUNTAINS

Yining

Urumqi
Tianchi L.
Mt. Bogda
Turpan
Jiaohe Ruins
Gaochang Ruins
Baicheng Kuqa
Aksu Kezi Thousand-Buddha Cave
Korla
Bosten L.

Tarim R.

Kashi Aitiduo Mosque
Mt. Kongur
Mt. Muztagata
Shache

Lop Nur
Loulan Ruins
Yumen Pass
Dunhuang Mogao Grottoes
Jiayuguan Pass

XINJIANG UYGUR AUT. REG.

ALTUN MOUNTAINS

QILIAN MOUNTAINS
Zhangye Great
Buddha Temple
Wester
M

GANSU

AFGHANISTAN

KASHMIR

Mt. Qogir

Hotian Yutian

KUNLUN MOUNTAINS

QINGHAI

Golmud

Qinghai L.

Birds Is
Xining
Ta'er Monastery
Lanz

PAKISTAN

Guge Kingdom Ruins

Guaring L.
Ngoring L.
Mt. A'nyemagen
Maiji Mountain

BAYAN HAR MOUNTAINS

TIBET AUT. REG.

GANGDISE MOUNTAINS

TANGGULA MOUNTAINS

Tongtian

Yalonghe

SICHUA

Jiuzhai Gully

NEW DELHI

HIMALAYA MOUNTAINS

Siling Co
Nam Co
Yangbajain
Potala Palace
Lhasa

Mt. Siguniang

Luding Bridge
Mt. Gongga Mt. Emei

HENGDUAN MOUNTAINS

I

N

D

I

A

NEPAL

Mount Xixabangma
Mount Qomolangma
Zhaxi Lhunbo Lamasery
Tibet Emperors' Tombs

SIKKIM BHUTAN

Den

Ganges

Tropic of Cancer

Ganges

BANGLADESH

INDIA

Three Rivers
Flow Togather
Lijiang Yulong
Snow Mountains

Dali The Third Day of
the Third Month Festival
Kunming

BURMA

Tengchong Terrestrial Heat
Dianchi L. Luna

YUNNAN

Xishuangbanna

LAOS

THAILAND

LEGEND

◎ Tourist City at Provincial Capital's Level

⊙ Tourist City below Provincial Capital's Level

● Tourist Area

▲ Famous Mountain and Snow-peak

SCALE

0   165   330   495   660 km

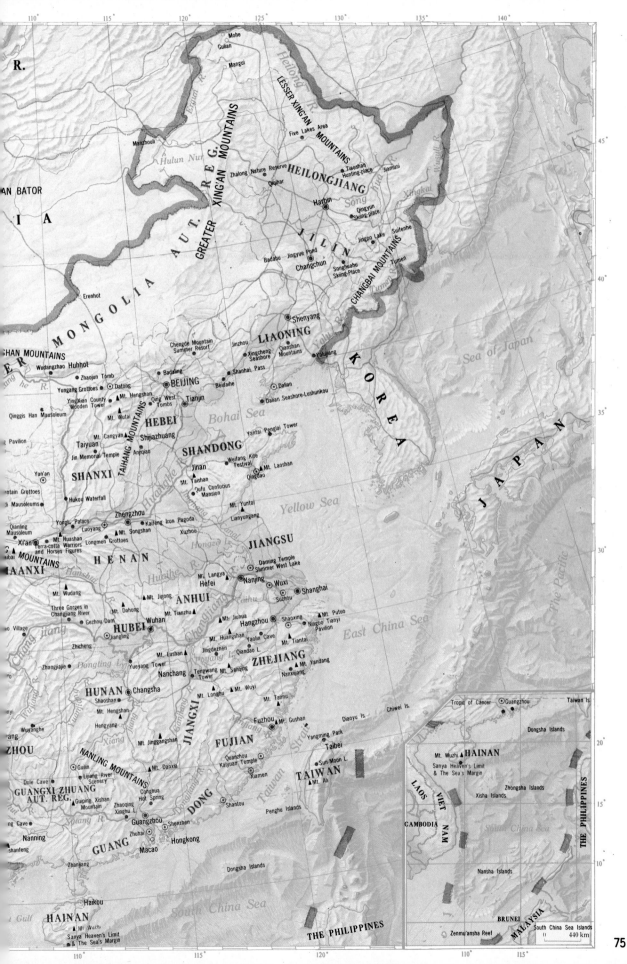

R.

MONGOLIA

AN BATOR

IA

Manzhouli

Erenhot

HAN MOUNTAINS

Wudangzhao Huhhot

Zhaojun Tomb

Yungang Grottoes Datong

Ying Xian County
Wooden Tower Mt. Hengshan

Qinggis Han Mausoleum

Mt. Wutai

Mt. Cangyan

HEBEI

Taiyuan Shijiazhuang

Jin Memorial Temple Anqiao

SHANXI

Yan'an

Huang he R.

ntain Grottoes

i Mausoleums Hukou Waterfall

Qianling
Mausoleum Yongle Palace Zhengzhou Kaifeng Iron Pagoda

Luoyang Mt. Songshan Xuzhou

Xi'an Longmen Grottoes

Terra-cotta Warriors
and Horses Figures

bai MOUNTAINS

AANXI HENAN

Hanshui R.

Mt. Wudang

Three Gorges in
Changjiang River Mt. Dahong Mt. Tianzhu

Gezhou Dam Wuhan

Zhicheng HUBEI Jiangling

o Village

Chang Jiang

Zhangjiajie Dongting Lu Yueyang Tower

HUNAN Nanchang

Shaoshan Changsha

Mt. Hengshan

nyi Hengyang

ZHOU Mt. Jinggangshan

NANLING MOUNTAINS

Wuyanghe Guilin

Dule Cave Lijiang River
Scenery

GUANGXI ZHUANG
AUT. REG. Guiping Xishan
Mountain Zhaoqing
Conghua
Hot Spring

ng Cave Xinghu L.

Guangzhou Shenzhen

Nanning Zhuhai

GUANG Macao Hongkong

shanfeng

Zhanjiang Dongsha Islands

HAINAN

Haikou

Mt. Wuzhi

Sanya Heaven's Limit
& The Sea's Margin

l Gulf South China Sea

THE PHILIPPINES

Mohe

Gulian

Mangui

Heilong R.

Ergun R.

GREATER XING'AN MOUNTAINS

Hulun Nur

LESSER XING'AN MOUNTAINS

Five Lakes Area

MOUNTAINS

Zhalong Nature Reserve Qiqihar HEILONGJIANG Tiaoshan
Hunting-place Jiamusi

Harbin

Qingyun
Skiing-Place

Jingpo Lake Suifenhe

JILIN

Badabu Jingyue Pond Changchun

Songhuahu
Skiing-Place Tumen

CHANGBAI MOUNTAINS

Shenyang

Chengde Mountain
Summer Resort Jinzhou LIAONING Qianshan
Mountains

Xingcheng
Seashore Yalujiang

KOREA

BEIJING Badaling Shanhai Pass

Beidaihe Dalian

Qing West
Tombs Tianjin Dalian Seashore-Lushunkou

Bohai Sea

SHANDONG Yantai Penglai Tower

Jinan Weifang Kite
Festival Mt. Laoshan

Mt. Taishan Qingdao

Qufu Confucius
Mansion

Mt. Yuntai

Lianyungang

Huanghe R.

JIANGSU

Daming Temple
Slimmer West Lake

Mt. Langya Nanjing Wuxi

Hefei Suzhou Shanghai

Mt. Jigong

ANHUI Hangzhou Mt. Putuo

Mt. Jiuhua Shaoxing Ningbo Tianyi
Pavilion

Mt. Huangshan Yaolin Cave

Jingdezhen Qiandao L. Mt. Tiantai

Lushan ZHEJIANG

Tengwang Mt. Sanqing Mt. Yandang
Tower

Mt. Longhu Nanxiang

Mt. Wuyi

JIANGXI Mt. Taimu

Mt. Danxia FUJIAN

Fuzhou Mt. Gushan

DONG Quanzhou
Kaiyuan Temple

Shantou Xiamen

Penghu Islands

Sea of Japan

Xinkai L.

Song Hua

Songhuahu

JAPAN

Yellow Sea

Hongze L.

Huaihe R.

Taihu

Poyang L.

East China Sea

The Pacific

Diaoyu Is. Chiwei Is.

Yangming Park

Taibei

TAIWAN Sun-Moon L.

Mt. Ali

Taiwan Strait

Dongsha Islands

Tropic of Cancer Guangzhou Taiwan Is.

Dongsha Islands

Mt. Wuzhi HAINAN

Sanya Heaven's Limit
& The Sea's Margin

Zhongsha Islands

Xisha Islands

LAOS VIET NAM

CAMBODIA

South China Sea

Nansha Islands

Zhenmu'ansha Reef

THE PHILIPPINES

BRUNEI

MALAYSIA

South China Sea Islands

0   440 km

Well-Known Historic Cultural Cities in China

Municipality   **Beijing, Shanghai, Tianjin**
Hebei Prov.   **Chengde, Baoding**
Shanxi Prov.   **Datong, Pingyao**
Inner Monggol Aut. Reg.   **Hohhot**
Liaoning Prov.   **Shenyang**
Shaanxi Prov.   **Xi'an, Yan'an, Hancheng, Yulin**
Gansu Prov.   **Wuwei, Zhangye, Dunhuang**
Ningxia Hui Aut. Reg.   **Yinchuan**
Xinjiang Uygur Aut. Reg.   **Kashi**
Shandong Prov.   **Qufu, Jinan**
Jiangsu Prov.   **Nanjing, Suzhou, Yangzhou, Zhenjiang, Changshu, Xuzhou, Huai'an**
Anhui Prov.   **Shexian, Shouxian, Bozhou**
Zhejiang Prov.   **Hangzhou, Shaoxing, Ningbo**

Jiangxi Prov.   **Jingdezhen, Nanchang**
Fujian Prov.   **Quanzhou, Fuzhou, Zhangzhou**
Henan Prov.   **Luoyang, Kaifeng, Anyang, Nanyang, Shangqiu**
Hubei Prov.   **Jiangling, Wuhan, Xiangfan**
Hunan Prov.   **Changsha**
Guangdong Prov.   **Guangzhou, Chaozhou**
Guangxi Zhuang Aut.Reg.   **Guilin**
Sichuan Prov.   **Chengdu, Chongqing, Langzhong, Yibin, Zigong**
Guizhou Prov.   **Zunyi, Zhenyuan**
Yunnan Prov.   **Kunming, Dali, Lijiang**
Xizang(Tibet) Aut. Reg.   **Lhasa, Xigaze**

Climate and Clothing

The major part of China is in the northern temperate zone with distinct seasons. So the weather is good for tourists all over the year. But the widespread of the land causes certain climate difference in various areas. Generally speaking, the southeast and central-south China is humid and rainy, while the north and northeast China is cold and dry.

In most areas tourists can wear light clothes (jacket or sweater) in spring (Mar.— May) and autum (Sept.— Nov.), and unlined garments in summer. But an overcoat is a must for outdoor use in winter. It frequently rains in May— June and Aug.—Sept., so raincoat is necessary for tourists in these periods of time.

The Average Temperature of the Major Tourist Cities in China (℃)

Month / City	Jan.	Feb.	Mar.	Apr.	May.	June.	July.	Aug.	Sept.	Oct.	Nov.	Dec.
Guangzhou	13.7	14.6	17.9	21.8	25.6	27.3	28.3	28.2	27.0	23.7	19.5	15.2
Fuzhou	10.5	10.7	13.4	18.2	22.1	25.5	28.8	28.2	26.0	21.7	17.5	13.1
Guilin	9.2	9.7	13.4	19.0	23.7	23.7	28.4	27.9	26.5	22.0	15.6	11.1
Guiyang	4.9	6.5	11.5	16.3	19.5	21.9	24.0	23.4	20.6	16.1	11.4	7.1
Kunming	7.7	9.6	13.0	16.5	19.1	19.5	19.8	19.1	17.5	14.9	11.3	8.2
Chongqing	8.1	9.7	14.1	18.8	22.7	25.1	28.7	28.8	24.2	18.7	14.2	9.9
Chengdu	5.5	7.5	12.1	17.8	20.9	23.7	25.6	25.1	21.2	16.8	11.9	7.3
Changsha	4.7	6.2	10.9	16.8	21.6	25.9	29.3	28.7	24.2	18.5	12.5	7.1
Nanchang	5.0	6.4	10.9	17.1	21.8	25.7	29.6	29.2	24.8	19.1	13.1	7.5
Wuhan	2.7	5.2	10.0	16.2	21.1	26.1	29.1	28.4	23.9	17.6	11.4	5.5
Hangzhou	3.8	5.1	9.3	15.4	20.2	24.3	28.6	28.0	23.3	17.7	12.1	6.5
Shanghai	3.5	4.9	8.2	13.7	18.6	23.4	28.0	27.6	23.5	17.8	12.5	6.2
Nanjing	2.0	3.8	8.4	14.8	19.9	24.5	28.0	27.8	22.7	16.9	10.5	4.4
Jinan	−4.4	1.1	7.6	15.2	21.8	26.3	27.4	26.2	21.7	15.8	7.8	1.1
Qingdao	−1.1	0.1	4.4	10.3	15.7	20.0	23.7	25.1	24.1	15.9	8.6	1.6
Tianjin	−4.0	−1.6	5.0	13.2	20.0	24.1	26.4	25.5	20.8	13.6	5.2	−1.6
Xi'an	−1.0	2.1	8.1	14.1	19.1	25.2	26.6	25.5	19.4	13.7	6.6	0.7
Lanzhou	−6.9	−2.3	5.2	11.8	16.6	20.3	22.2	21.0	15.8	9.4	1.7	−5.5
Urumqi	−15.4	−12.1	−4.0	9.0	15.9	21.2	23.5	22.0	16.8	7.4	−4.2	−11.6
Shenyang	−12.0	−8.4	0.1	9.3	16.9	21.5	24.6	23.5	17.2	9.4	0.0	−8.5
Changchun	−16.4	−12.7	−3.5	6.7	15.0	20.1	23.0	21.3	15.0	6.8	−3.8	−12.8
Harbin	−19.4	−15.4	−4.8	6.0	14.3	20.0	22.8	21.1	14.4	5.6	−5.7	−15.6

INDEX

Friends !

Welcome to Beijing !

The Happiest Memories of

the Charming City Will

Accompany You Forever !

TOURIST ATLAS OF BEIJING

Consultants	Bo Xicheng,　Liao Ke,　Chen Zhiping, Lu Bing
Editor—in—chief	Qian Jinkai
Members of the Editorial Broad	Lu Renwei,　Du Guangbo,　Shi Zuhui, Liu Qinyu,　Yao Suihan,　Zhang Jianyi, Qian Jinkai
Editors and Cartographers	Qian Jinkai,　Wei Fang
Article Writer	Liu Qinyu
Translators	Yang Zhouhuai,　Gao Guopei
Designer of Front Cover	Zhang Baohua
Photographers	Te Yongcai, Deng Yongqing, E'Yi, Gao Chunduan, Zhang Jianyi, Wang Chunshu, Zhang Zhaoji, Sun Yongxue, Sun Shuqing, Liu Wenmin, Liu Chen, Liu Qijun, Xie Jun, Wei Mingxiang, Yang Xiuyun, Wang Zhengbao, Ma Jun
Responsible Editors	Yao Suihan, Li Bin